BRABHAM BT52

1983 (all models)

COVER CUTAWAY: Brabham BT52. *(Sergio Baratto)*

First published in January 2016

A catalogue record for this book is available from the British Library.

ISBN 978 0 85733 820 4

Library of Congress control no. 2014957452

Published by Haynes Publishing,
Sparkford, Yeovil,
Somerset BA22 7JJ, UK.
Tel: 01963 440635
Int. tel: +44 1963 440635
Website: www.haynes.co.uk

Haynes North America Inc.,
861 Lawrence Drive, Newbury Park,
California 91320, USA.

Printed in the USA by
Odcombe Press LP,
1299 Bridgestone Parkway,
La Vergne, TN 37086.

Acknowledgements

This book would not have been possible without the help of many people. I would like to thank all of the following for their assistance in helping to bring this book to life.

Mauro Baldi
Rebecca Banks
Herbie Blash
Charles Bradley
Robert Dean
Pierre Dupasquier
Teo Fabi
Roberto Guerrero
Carlos Jalife
Davy Jones
Raimund Kupferschmid
Bruce MacIntosh
Heini Mader
Rupert Manwaring
Gordon Murray
Jack Nicholls
David North
Riccardo Patrese
Anthony Peacock
Nelson Piquet
Andy Pope
Hector Rebaque
Paul Rosche
Sam Smith
Harvey Spencer
Edd Straw
John Townsend
Roly Vincini
Gary Watkins
Charlie Whiting

BRABHAM BT52

1983 (all models)

Owners' Workshop Manual

An insight into the design, engineering, maintenance and operation of Brabham's BMW-turbo-powered F1 car

Andrew van de Burgt

Contents

OPPOSITE The dramatic-looking BT52 stunned the paddock when Brabham unveiled the car ahead of the 1983 season.
(Dirk Daniel Mann/BMW)

RIGHT BMW's straight-four turbocharged engine was the most powerful to ever be used in F1, with over 1,400bhp.
(Dirk Daniel Mann/BMW)

Chapter One

The Brabham story

The Brabham name remains one of the most famous in motorsport despite the fact it has been 30 years since a car bearing that name won a grand prix and more than 20 years since one even started a grand prix.

The history of this great marque can be broken down into three distinct periods – the Jack Brabham years, the Bernie Ecclestone years and the 'Wilderness' years.

OPPOSITE Jack Brabham (1) leads team-mate Denny Hulme (2) in the 1967 British GP at Silverstone. *(LAT)*

The Jack Brabham years

Born in Hurstville near Sydney in 1926, John Arthur 'Jack' Brabham developed an interest in cars at a young age, and went on to study technical drawing and metalwork at college. On his 18th birthday he enlisted in the Royal Australian Air Force, where he became a flight mechanic. He had attained the rank of leading aircraftman by the time he was discharged in 1946.

Back in the civilian world, he put his mechanical skills to use and opened up a repair shop in the grounds of his grandfather's house. It was through his work here on the JAP engine of American Jonny Schonberg's midget racer that he became introduced to the world of motorsport. When, in 1948, Schonberg ceded to pressure from his wife and stopped racing, Brabham took over his car.

Brabham proved to be a natural, winning on just his third night on the dirt ovals and going on to win the Australian Speedcar Championship that year. Revelling in the heat of combat and living on his lightning-quick reactions, success continued to flow.

In 1951 Brabham tried his hand at hillclimbing, which led to an interest in road racing and a relationship with the Cooper Car Company, from whom he had purchased some cars for his racing exploits. Soon Brabham started to replicate on road courses the success he had achieved in midget racing. His dark hair, thick stubble and ruthless approach earned him the nickname 'Black Jack'.

After starring in the 1955 New Zealand Grand Prix, Brabham was persuaded by Dean Delamont, the competitions manager of the Royal Automobile Club, to head to Europe and pit his skills against the leading lights of the day.

Moving to the UK allowed Jack to forge a strong relationship with Charles Cooper and his son John. Before long he had become an unofficial employee. Using his skills as a mechanic, he actually built the 2-litre single-seat Bobtail in which he made his Formula 1 début at the 1955 British Grand Prix.

The streamlined little car, with its enclosed wheels, was too under-powered to compete at the front in Formula 1 in Europe, but when Brabham shipped it back to Australia for that year's Australian Grand Prix, it proved to be good enough to win the race. This achievement led to Brabham selling the car, which funded a full-time move to the UK for him and his family.

While Brabham had success in Formula 2 and sports cars, it wasn't until Cooper obtained the 2.5-litre Climax engine for the 1959 season that he was able to show his true pace in the premier class of motor racing. Victory at

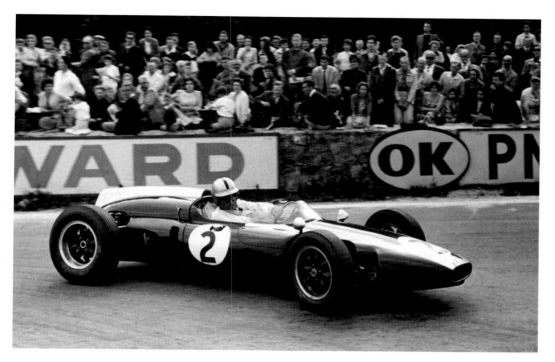

Monaco and Aintree and a famous fourth place at Sebring, where he pushed the car over the line after it ran out of fuel on the final lap, secured him the World Championship title.

Yet despite the success, Brabham was convinced he could do better. His friend and countryman Ron Tauranac had joined him in the UK and through Jack Brabham Motors they had already started to design upgrade kits for British road cars such as the Sunbeam Rapier. Retirement from the season-opening Argentinian Grand Prix in 1960 led to a frank exchange with John Cooper, and thereafter Brabham was permitted to make changes to the cars that the Coopers had been reluctant to implement. With input from Tauranac, the result was the Cooper T53. Brabham spun on its début at Monaco, but then embarked upon a remarkable run of five straight wins and another World Championship crown was secured.

Formula 1 rules changed for 1961, with engine size reduced to 1.5 litres. With Ferrari finally having adopted Cooper's rear-engine approach and Coventry Climax running behind schedule with the new engine that most of the British teams would use, the T55 was out-classed that year and Brabham was a distant 11th in the World Championship.

Mid-season, Brabham and Tauranac formed Motor Racing Developments (MRD). Its first product was a Formula Junior car – the BT1. Just one was built, but it paved the way for the BT2, 11 of which are believed to have been made and sold around the world.

In 1962 Motor Racing Developments also produced the BT3, a Formula 1 car that Brabham raced himself through the Brabham Racing Organisation. In just its third race, Brabham took his self-built Formula 1 car to third place in the non-championship Oulton Park Gold Cup, while its first World Championship points followed with fourth place in the US Grand Prix at Watkins Glen.

BELOW John Cooper (right) congratulates Brabham after victory in the 1960 British GP at Silverstone. *(LAT)*

ABOVE Dan Gurney scored the first win for a Brabham F1 car in the 1964 French GP. *(LAT)*

LEFT The 1966 F1 title celebrated in style with an ice cream replica of the winning car. *(LAT)*

Business grew at MRD and in 1963 there were 20 BT2s built alongside two BT7 Formula 1 cars as American Dan Gurney joined as Brabham's team-mate. It was Gurney who recorded the marque's first win, taking the chequered flag in the 1964 French Grand Prix at Rouen. Brabham diced with BRM's Graham Hill behind him, eventually coming home third.

Gurney would win again at the season finale in Mexico, but poor reliability cost him any chance of the title. It was not until 1966 and a change to the 3-litre engine formula that Brabham produced a title challenger.

Having persuaded Australian engineering specialist Repco to build a V8 engine around Oldsmobile's aluminium-alloy 215 engine, Brabham had an engine that made up for its

LEFT Brabham also starred in Formula 2. Here he is with team-mate Denny Hulme after a 1–2 at Pau in 1966. *(LAT)*

relative lack of power by being reliable and light in weight.

The combination worked beautifully. Brabham won the French Grand Prix at Reims, the first of four successive wins that carried him to his third World Championship title. It made him the first – and so far only – man to win the Formula 1 World Championship in a car bearing his own name. Underlining just what a force Brabham had become as both constructor and driver, he also dominated Formula 2 that year, winning 10 of 16 races in the Honda-powered BT18, although there was no official championship in place.

Brabham continued its success into 1967, but this time it was Denny Hulme who won the World Championship. The Kiwi enjoyed superior reliability to his team-mate, whose desire to try new parts is often said to have been the reason for him missing out on a fourth World Championship title.

Poor reliability continued to plague Brabham in 1968, while a testing accident midway through 1969 resulted in a seriously injured foot. This prompted him to sell his share of the team to Tauranac and to promise his wife Betty that he would retire at the end of the season.

But with the team unable to find a top-line replacement for Jochen Rindt, who had moved to Lotus, and Jacky Ickx, who had joined Ferrari, Brabham opted to carry on driving into 1970. Victory in the South African Grand Prix, aged 44, vindicated his decision.

Following his retirement, Brabham returned to Australia to live on a farm and raise his three sons – Geoff, Gary and David – all of whom went on to enjoy successful racing careers. Jack never raced again, although he made numerous guest appearances at events around the world until ill health meant he could no longer travel. He received an OBE in 1966 and became the first racing driver to be knighted in 1979. He died peacefully in 2014 aged 88.

ABOVE Brabham talks to mechanic Ron Dennis (right), the man who would go on to run the McLaren empire. *(LAT)*

BELOW Brabham's final season behind the wheel was in 1970, when he was still a winner aged 44. *(LAT)*

ABOVE Young Argentinian Carlos Reutemann joined Brabham for 1972, but the team was not a frontrunner. *(LAT)*

BELOW The striking BT42 was the first Brabham Gordon Murray created as the team's chief designer. *(LAT)*

The Bernie Ecclestone years

Following Sir Jack's retirement at the end of the 1970 season, Tauranac owned and ran Brabham by himself. While Formula 1 results in 1971 were disappointing, with just a single podium finish for Tim Schencken in the BT33 in Austria, Motor Racing Developments was still a force as a constructor, building 27 of its BT35C Formula 3 cars alongside Formula Atlantic and hillclimb cars. But all that was about to change…

During the 1971 season, Tauranac approached Bernie Ecclestone to become a business partner in Brabham. Ecclestone ultimately persuaded Tauranac to sell him the entire team for £100,000. Initially Tauranac stayed on as designer, but the relationship was never destined to last and he left early in the 1972 season.

Brabham spent a year in the doldrums in 1972, but Ecclestone's decision to promote young South African Gordon Murray to chief designer was almost instantly rewarded. Murray's attractive, angular BT42 made its début four races into the season and quickly proved itself to be superior to the out-going BT37, taking its first podium finish in the hands of Carlos Reutemann at the French Grand Prix.

During 1973 the last of the non-Formula 1 Brabhams – the BT41 Formula 3 car – was built. For 1974 Formula 1 would be the sole

BELOW In 1975 the BT44B took the fight to Ferrari. Carlos Pace is shown at speed at the Nürburgring. *(LAT)*

focus and Brabham returned to the winner's circle when Reutemann won the tragic South African Grand Prix in the stunning BT44, taking advantage of Niki Lauda's late mechanical problems to claim his first Formula 1 win. Reutemann won again at the Österreichring and Watkins Glen, but his poor finishing record at the start of the season meant he was a distant fifth in the final standings.

The car was evolved into the BT44B for 1975 and reliability was much improved. Either Reutemann or team-mate Carlos Pace finished on the podium in each of the opening seven races, which including an emotional home win for Pace in the Brazilian Grand Prix. Yet despite this, neither driver was a match for Lauda and Ferrari, who romped to the World Championship.

Ecclestone signed a lucrative deal with Alfa Romeo to use its engines for 1976. But the Italian flat-12 was heavy, thirsty and under-powered compared with the Ford-Cosworth DFV it replaced. Reutemann was gone from the team before the end of the season – to replace the injured Lauda at Ferrari – while Pace scored just three top-six finishes.

While still overweight, the Alfa engine was at least more powerful for 1977, allowing John Watson to put the BT45 on the front row for its début in Argentina. Despite leading four races, however, 'Wattie' did not manage to win that year.

ABOVE John Watson leads the 1977 British GP, but victory eluded him and the BT45 that season. *(LAT)*

BELOW World Champion Niki Lauda joined Brabham for 1978 and won twice, including here at Monza. *(LAT)*

ABOVE The BT53 of 1984 was fast, but unreliable. New driver Teo Fabi would score just nine points. *(LAT)*

It was not until Sweden in 1978 and the controversial BT46B 'fan car' that a Brabham won again, with Lauda at the wheel, the Austrian having joined the team for the 1978 season after falling out with Ferrari. With the rival teams staggered by Lauda's margin of victory in Sweden, there was considerable pressure for the fan concept to be banned. Reluctantly, Ecclestone consented to shelving the project, but in doing so he secured the agreement of his competitors to join the Formula One Constructors' Association (FOCA) that he had

RIGHT With Pirelli tyres, Piquet struggled in 1985, but he dominated the French GP in the BT54. *(LAT)*

founded, a move that ultimately paved the way to him becoming the most powerful man in Formula 1.

Lauda won again in the conventional BT46 at Monza, but the upturn in performance was not sustained and repeated engine woes were among the factors that ultimately drove Lauda into retirement midway through the 1979 season. That year a young Brazilian called Nelson Piquet joined the team, having come into Formula 1 on the back of winning the 1978 BP Formula 3 Championship. With three races of the 1979 season remaining, Alfa decided to concentrate on building cars of its own and the relationship with Brabham was terminated.

With a Cosworth DFV in the back, the new BT49 – in new blue and white Parmalat livery – was instantly more competitive and Piquet was able to challenge for the 1980 World Championship title. A year later, driving in the updated BT49C, the Brazilian finally became the third Brabham driver to win the World Championship crown.

By this time the writing was on the wall for the DFV as the mighty turbos from Renault and Ferrari found the reliability to match their awesome power. During his title-winning season Piquet tested a car fitted with a BMW four-cylinder turbo engine, and even though reliability was suspect, he enthusiastically backed the decision to campaign the turbo BT50 in 1982, while team-mate Riccardo Patrese initially relied on the proven 'atmospheric' BT49D, which he used to win the Monaco Grand Prix.

Such was the difficulty of taming the power of the turbo that Piquet failed to qualify for the Detroit race, but he rebounded in style to win the Canadian Grand Prix the following weekend to record BMW's first Formula 1 win.

A late change in regulations meant Brabham had to abandon its BT51 design and produce the BT52 at record speed. The result was a stunning-looking car that is the focus of this book.

The BT53 of 1984 was equally gorgeous but fragile. Despite Piquet setting nine pole positions, he claimed just two wins as the McLarens of Alain Prost and Lauda dominated. A deal to run on Pirelli tyres was agreed for 1985, but it proved to be a disaster. With the

LEFT The low-line
concept of the BT55
was not a success,
but Murray replicated
the idea at McLaren
in the form of the
all-conquering 1988
MP4/4. (LAT)

exception of the French Grand Prix, which Piquet ran away with, the BT54 was seldom a front-runner.

For 1986 Piquet departed for Williams, and a king's ransom. Patrese returned to Brabham and was joined by fellow Italian Elio de Angelis. Murray designed a radical 'low-line' car – the BT55 – but it was beset from the start by technical issues. A terrible season for the team was compounded when de Angelis was killed in a testing accident at Paul Ricard.

The conventional BT56 returned Brabham to the podium in the hands of Andrea de Cesaris in the 1987 San Marino Grand Prix. But this was a season ruined by engine unreliability as BMW would only supply the 'lie-down' version built for the BT55.

By this time Murray had departed for McLaren and Ecclestone was becoming increasingly powerful through his position at the head of FOCA. When no engine partner could be found to replace BMW, Brabham missed the deadline to appear on the 1988 Formula 1 entry list, and ahead of the season opener in

BELOW The BT56 of 1987 was the last Brabham F1 car to be created with the team under Bernie Ecclestone's ownership. (LAT)

to Walter Brun, the Austrian slot-machine millionaire who had entered Formula 1 that season with his EuroBrun outfit.

The 'Wilderness' years

Before the 1989 season had even started Walter Brun sold Brabham to Swiss businessman Joachim Lüthi. Although the team was required to pre-qualify, the Sergio Rinland-designed, Judd-powered BT58 was a good car, and Stefano Modena and Martin Brundle were able to hustle it into positions that embarrassed better-funded rivals. Modena was third at Monaco, a race that Brundle could have won but for a battery problem. That season the team scored eight points – the most the reborn marque would register.

The Brabham revival was stopped in its tracks when Lüthi was arrested for tax evasion. The team was taken over by Japanese investment group Middlebridge, but funds were limited and so were results, although there was history resonance when Sir Jack's youngest son, David, qualified the BT59 for the 1990 Monaco Grand Prix. Brundle returned for 1991 to drive the Yamaha-powered BT60Y, an uncompetitive car/ engine package but nonetheless one that he did manage to drag into the points at Suzuka, as did team-mate Mark Blundell at Spa. Brundle's fifth place in Japan turned out to be the last time a Brabham car finished in the points.

Brazil Ecclestone finally confirmed that Brabham would be absent from the grid for the first time since 1960.

During 1988 the remaining Brabham employees were kept busy building the Alfa Romeo 164 Procar (code-named BT57) that made a single, devastating appearance at the 1988 Italian Grand Prix. It was suggested that its staggering performance frightened off the opposition, but, regardless of the truth, the fact is that this Procar series never happened.

Ecclestone sold Motor Racing Developments

With finances exceedingly tight, Brabham's drivers struggled to get the Judd-powered BT60B even through qualifying in 1992. Initially Eric van de Poele and female racer Giovanna Amati were given the unenviable task of trying to qualify, which van de Poele managed only at the season opener in South Africa. Amati tried three times, without success, and her non-qualification for the Brazilian Grand Prix was the last time a woman attempted to start a Formula 1 race. Her place was taken by Damon Hill, who finally made the cut – after five unsuccessful attempts – at the British Grand Prix. Van de Poele left the team ahead of the Hungarian Grand Prix, where Hill once again qualified.

After that race Brabham disappeared from Formula 1, with Middlebridge unable to pay its debts and its creditors, Landhurst Leasing, under investigation by the Serious Fraud Office. Following four drivers' titles, two constructors' titles and 35 wins, it was a sad and ignominious end to one of the sport's greatest marques.

ABOVE Giovanna Amati was the last woman to attempt to race in F1 when she drove for Brabham in 1992. *(LAT)*

LEFT Damon Hill made his F1 debut for Brabham in 1992. A year later he was winning races for Williams. *(LAT)*

Chapter Two

Design and development of the Brabham BT52

The Brabham BT52, designed by Gordon Murray with David North, was a radical rethink that built upon knowledge gained during the ground-effect era and the growing potency and reliability of BMW's turbo engine. The two breakthrough concepts introduced to it were mid-race refuelling – the car had a smaller fuel tank than its predecessors – and significantly more rearward weight distribution in order to improve traction at this time of ever-increasing turbo power outputs.

OPPOSITE Piquet at ten tenths during the opening stages of the South African GP as he established a huge lead and broke his rivals. *(John Townsend)*

19

ABOVE Bernie Ecclestone (right) and Colin Chapman – two of the most influential figures in the history of Formula 1. *(LAT)*

In the nascent days of motorsport, the quest for speed was inextricably linked to power. In order to go faster, engines became bigger and more powerful. Supercharging took this even further, to the point where Auto Union's cars were developing well over 500bhp before the Second World War. Two more generations would pass before these power levels were exceeded in Formula 1.

As racing returned to a war-ravaged Europe, initially the cars, unsurprisingly, were based on the technology that had existed before hostilities. This meant that the pursuit of power – albeit within more tightly defined regulations – prevailed, but not for long. While the big German, Italian and French manufacturers were playing the power game, a new breed of British privateer was exploring the benefits of handling.

Lotus and Cooper developed their tiny cars, with the engine mounted behind the driver instead of in front, and took on the big boys. While success came pretty quickly in Formula 2 and sports-car racing, in Formula 1 brute force still held sway. But when Stirling Moss took the chequered flag at the 1958 Argentine Grand Prix in Rob Walker's mid-engined Cooper T43, the tide was about to turn. By the time an exhausted Jack Brabham pushed his Cooper T51 over the line at Sebring to win the 1959 Formula 1 World Championship, the sea change was well under way. While power would always be desirable, now it was handling that was the holy grail of racing-car design.

The next major step in the search for better handling was the arrival of aerofoil wings, which Lotus first introduced on the 49 midway through 1968 and were almost instantly copied by the rest of the paddock. At a time when technology was taking men into space and ultimately to the moon, and through the sound barrier on passenger flights, advances in aerodynamic understanding came on in leaps and bounds from the fragile-looking strut-mounted wings of the pioneering Lotus design.

Ground effect

Lotus again led the way with the 72, which heralded the arrival of the concept known as ground effect. This car's wedge-like shape, narrow track and inboard brakes caught the eye, but it was what was happening to the air going underneath that distinctive pointed nose that was to have a lasting legacy. The concept of ground effect – creating and enhancing downforce by accelerating the airflow between the ground and the lower surface of the car – had first been explored by McLaren on its M6 sports car, which ran in the North American Can-Am series.

It may have been unintentional, but a recent Computational Fluid Dynamics (CFD) study of the 72 demonstrated that its nose did indeed create an area of low pressure that sucked the car to the ground – ie, it had ground effect. This information was published in Mark Hughes's book *F1 Retro: 1970*, in which Gordon McCabe commented: '…demonstrates that low pressure is created at the front of the 72 by both the lower surface of the wing elements, and by the acceleration of air under the wedge-shaped nose itself. Whilst the pressure minimum lies under the front of the nose, a region of moderately reduced underbody pressure extends rearwards between the front wheels. The Lotus 72 therefore generated some of its front downforce by ground effect.'

With the 72 taking Lotus to the Formula 1 drivers' championship in 1970 (Jochen Rindt) and 1972 (Emerson Fittipaldi), the onus was now on the other teams to understand how this downforce was being achieved and to find ways to harness it more effectively.

GORDON MURRAY – CHIEF DESIGNER

Born in Durban, South Africa to Scottish parents, Gordon Murray moved to England in 1969 to pursue his love of racing cars. A meeting with Ron Tauranac led to a job at Brabham and when Tauranac left to form Ralt, new Brabham owner Bernie Ecclestone made Murray chief designer.

Murray established a reputation for designing beautiful-looking cars that pushed the regulations to the limits – or 'finding the unfair advantage' as he describes it. His Brabhams won the drivers' World Championship in 1981 and 1983, but with Ecclestone's attentions becoming diverted away from Brabham and more towards the running of Formula 1, Murray moved to McLaren to become its technical director in 1987.

Under his stewardship, the McLaren team produced the MP4/4, which won 15 of 16 races in 1988. After more titles in 1989, 1990 and 1991, Murray went on to establish McLaren Cars, which produced the legendary F1 supercar and its Le Mans-winning race version as well as the Mercedes-Benz McLaren SLR.

Murray left McLaren in 2004 and in 2007 established Gordon Murray Design (GMD). Based in Surrey, GMDfd has a number of high-profile clients in the automotive world and recently confirmed that it is involved in a project to resurrect the TVR sports-car brand.

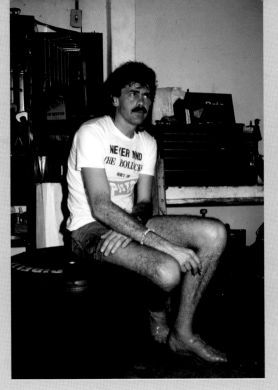

LEFT The Sex Pistols T-shirt says it all – Murray always took an anarchic approach to the F1 rulebook. *(John Townsend)*

LEFT Murray was hands on at the track too, discussing strategy and set-up with lead driver Nelson Piquet. *(LAT)*

LEFT Murray and pattern maker Mike Reid stand outside the 'yellow submarine' autoclave at Chessington. *(LAT)*

ABOVE Lauda dominated the 1978 Swedish GP with the BT46B 'fan car'. *(LAT)*

At Brabham Gordon Murray had been promoted to chief designer after Ron Tauranac left to set up Ralt. Murray's first car in his new role was the BT42, which made its début midway through the 1973 season. Like the Lotus 72, it was a handsome, wedge-like creation but it was its successor, the BT44 of 1974, that featured the addition of a plastic 'skirt'. This piece of plastic, which was attached to the base of the bodywork and ran to the ground,

helped to seal the air under the car, while air dams at the front of the car forced out the air to create an area of low pressure that sucked the car to the ground.

The theory behind the use of skirts is that they shield the low-pressure area created under the car from the high-pressure air formed by the drag over the upper surfaces of the car. This was a phenomenon first observed on the tips of aeroplane wings – the lessons learned from the aviation world were starting to be taken into racing-car design.

With the 78, Lotus developed what became known as a 'wing car'. The car leaned heavily on fluid dynamic theory, using the shape of the underside of the radiators to create an upturned aeroplane wing. It effectively turned the whole underside of the car into a big wing, which forced the car towards the track.

BELOW The fan was used to suck the air from under the car to create enormous downforce. *(LAT)*

BELOW RIGHT Fan technology was banned after a single race, so its full potential was never realised. *(LAT)*

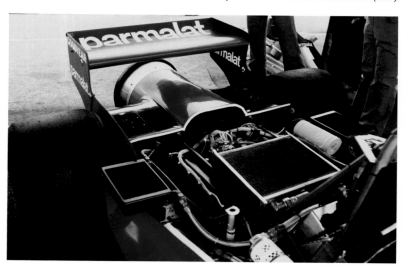

The concept was refined for the 79, which Mario Andretti and Ronnie Peterson used to dominate the 1978 World Championship. The only serious competition came from another of Murray's creations, the BT46B 'fan car', which Niki Lauda took to victory in the Swedish Grand Prix.

This 'fan car' took the notion of creating a low-pressure area under the car to the extreme by using a fan to suck away the air. Despite the car being a compromised evolution of the standard BT46, it was an overwhelming success, as Lauda dominated the race at Anderstorp, winning by over half a minute. The true potential of the fan concept was never explored as the technology was outlawed in the wake of this rout.

By 1979 all the teams had a version of a wing car, some of which were more successful than others. But the ones that worked, such as the Williams FW07 and Brabham BT49, refined the concept to an amazing degree. Such was the grip that the ground effect was now generating, the cars had more than two tonnes of downforce to help them literally 'fly' around corners. Indeed they had so much grip that often teams were able to run without front wings at all.

The early 1980s was a tumultuous period in Formula 1 history. A war between the governing body FISA (now the FIA) and the teams' body FOCA had broken out over the way the sport was run, how money was distributed and how the rules were made.

There were numerous flashpoints as the conflict escalated from a war of words. The first of these took place in 1980, when some drivers from FOCA-affiliated teams were fined for non-

ABOVE with the DFV replacing the Alfa V12s, Brabham introduced the BT49 towards the end of 1979. *(LAT)*

LEFT Piquet won three races with the BT49 in 1980 and narrowly missed out on the World Championship. *(LAT)*

attendance of the drivers' briefings at previous races. With their licences suspended pending the payments of fines, a stalemate was reached prior to the Spanish Grand Prix. This was only broken when the race went ahead without the sanctioning of FISA, which led to it being declared a non-championship event.

The following year, when FISA fell out with the organisers of the South African Grand Prix over the date of the race, FOCA created the World Federation of Motorsport and held the race on the original date, but with only the FOCA-affiliated teams taking part. However, the event was not a success and peace was made, and the breakaway threat subsided.

In the run-up to the 1982 season the prospect of a drivers' strike was only narrowly averted. The dispute centred around a clause inserted by FISA into the drivers' contracts stating that they could only race for the team with which they had started the season. It was only when this was withdrawn on the eve of the South African Grand Prix that the rift was healed.

Just a few months later the FOCA teams boycotted the San Marino Grand Prix, with the consequence that only 14 cars started the race and just six finished (and one of those was subsequently disqualified). The boycott arose as a result of the disqualification of Nelson Piquet and Keke Rosberg from the season-opening Brazilian Grand Prix, where Brabham and Williams (both FOCA-affiliated teams) ran water-cooled brakes; the water for this system was supplied from ballast tanks and when, post-race, FISA refused to allow these tanks to be refilled, both cars were declared underweight.

The Brazilian race was held in sweltering conditions. Piquet and Rosberg were exhausted when they appeared on the podium, while Piquet's Brabham team-mate, Riccardo Patrese, withdrew from the race through fatigue. The sheer amount of downforce generated by the cars was a factor, as the physical strength and energy needed to race them for two hours was extreme.

That 1982 season was also a tragic one. Ferrari's hugely popular lead driver Gilles Villeneuve was killed in qualifying for the Belgian Grand Prix. Osella's Italian rookie Riccardo Paletti succumbed to the terrible injuries he sustained when he ran into the back of Didier Pironi's stalled Ferrari at the start of the Canadian Grand Prix and his car burst into flames. Pironi himself suffered career-ending injuries when he vaulted over the rear of Alain Prost's Renault in wet practice for the German Grand Prix.

In light of all these events a change to the regulations was inevitable. It is debatable whether or not the decision to effectively outlaw ground effect – by banning skirts and mandating a flat bottom to the cars – was politically motivated to penalise the FOCA teams, but it is certainly true that the Cosworth-powered 'FOCA cars' were able to get more out of the ground-effect concept than their turbocharged rivals, the majority of whom were in the FISA camp. The impact, nevertheless, was challenging for all. The timing of the decision – the 1983 rules were only made official in late October 1982 – meant a considerable headache for all the teams in order to have their new cars ready in time for the first grand prix of the following year, in Brazil on 13 March.

Following a meeting of the FISA Executive Committee in Paris on 11–13 October 1982, the following statement was made, as quoted in *Autosport*.

Due to a case of force majeure *and for the safety of the drivers and the spectators the following modifications to the Formula 1 World Championship Technical Regulations shall come into force on January 1, 1983 or as from the first official European Grand Prix, if the constructors request this from the FISA.*

1. *Introduction of a full flat bottom of the car between the rear tangent of the front wheels and the front tangent of the rear wheels*
2. *Banning of skirts and any systems used to fill the gap between the bodywork and the ground*
3. *Height of the rear wing increased by 10cms to increase rear visibility of the driver*
4. *Reduction of the width of the rear wing from 110cms to 100cms and of the overhang from 80cms to 60cms to reduce the aerodynamic downforce*
5. *Increase in the frontal protection of the drivers' feet from 30cms to 50cms (survival cell)*
6. *Improvement of the tank protection and the side panels of the car*
7. *Improvement of the rear red lights (power increased from 15 to 25 watts)*
8. *New system of checking the weight of the cars during practice, at the entrance to the pits and after the race*
9. *New definition of the weight of the car (the minimum weight is the weight of the car with the petrol on board, in order to simplify checks)*
10. *Minimum weight: 540kgs*
11. *Banning of four-wheel-drive cars*
12. *Banning of cars with more than four wheels*
13. *Obligation for the competitor to prove eligibility of his car(s) to the scrutineers*

ABOVE Murray designed the BT51 to ground-effect rules, which meant the car was ineligible for the 1983 season. *(LAT)*

At the time, a clearly exasperated Murray told *Autosport*: 'It's got to the point where we don't care anymore – we are happy as long as we have some regulations. We have redrawn our car so many times to rumoured regulations we got fed up.

'These regulations will slow the cars down but I can't say whether they will be safer. I would say that you have got to have a turbo, though. We are having a planning meeting now to decide how to tackle the problem. It will require a whole new car and it will be a couple of weeks before I can say when we would be ready to run.'

As Murray explained, in lieu of any fixed rules, he had had no choice but to design a car for 1983 based around what he thought the regulations would be. This was the BT51.

Visually very similar to the Brabham BT49D that had been raced during 1982, the BT51 was

BELOW The BT51 tested numerous times during 1982 and early 1983 but would never be raced. *(LAT)*

designed around the concept of full ground effect. Thus it had the full-length sidepods needed to create the large floor surface where the low-pressure area would suck the car to the ground.

So far did this project advance that two full chassis were built. They were tested (without skirts) at Paul Ricard in November 1982 (and again throughout the winter), even though the rules had been changed, rendering them obsolete at this point. Both BT51s were subsequently scrapped at the behest of Brabham team boss Bernie Ecclestone, making the design one of the intriguing 'lost' Formula 1 cars that were built but never raced.

Only the wheels and pedals from the BT51 were carried over to the BT52, which Murray and his assistant David North designed at record speed.

'We'd done all this work based on the bloody BT51,' Murray recalls. 'There was only David North and me in the design office. We did a lot of work and I was engineering both cars at the race track still in those days. I had a season's worth of work and on top of that had to design the car in the middle of the season, so I was knackered!

'I had to start again in October time, with a completely different car with no skirts. I ended up by working the most ridiculous hours. I went to the doctor and I lived on pills for about three months as I designed that car. So that was the background to the BT52!'

The removal of skirts meant far more than just cosmetic alteration. This was a fundamental change in the design philosophy of the car.

'The problem I had was that I knew with

skirts, when we were producing the BT49, that we were generating 2.5 tonnes of downforce at top speed and if you got the centre of pressure wrong by 10mm, the car wouldn't handle in high-speed corners. So I knew with the BT51 I would have to do a lot of very delicate work with the sidepod profile and other stuff, which is one of the reasons that I did it early. When you lost a skirt, I had no idea where the centre of pressure was going to go. And I knew I had no time to develop in the wind tunnel a proper sidepod, so rather than do that I just dumped the sidepods altogether. I just took a massive decision to go "we're not doing sidepods".'

Turbocharging

While turbocharging had been commonplace in Indycar and sports-car racing since the late 1960s, with Porsche in particular enjoying tremendous success with its 1,000bhp+ 917/10 Can-Am car, it was not until 1977 that the technology entered Formula 1, courtesy of Renault.

At first the cars were very unreliable, but by 1979 they were able to show their full potential on tracks where top speed was more important than traction, such as Dijon. By 1980 Renault was winning races on a regular basis and a switch to turbocharged engines was being contemplated throughout the paddock. Ferrari introduced its V6 turbo in 1981, while a new British team, Toleman, entered the fray with a four-cylinder turbo built by engine specialist Brian Hart.

In essence the rules had reverted Formula

1 to its original ethos. Once again it would be power that ruled. And with the turbocharged engines now comfortably surpassing those amazing power figures of the Auto Union, the main job of the chassis now was to harness the power of this new breed of flame-spitting 1.5-litre powerplants.

The potential of the turbo engine led Bernie Ecclestone to sign a deal in the middle of 1980 for a supply of engines from BMW. The German manufacturer had introduced its first turbocharged road car – the 2002 Turbo – in 1973, and had enjoyed success with a racing version of its engine installed in the subsequent 320 model in German touring cars and IMSA racing in the US.

At the behest of Jochen Neerpasch, BMW's Competition Manager, work then began on investigating the suitability of the engine for racing in Formula 1. According to Alan Henry's book *Brabham: The Grand Prix Cars*, Neerpasch proposed a BMW engine deal with Niki Lauda and McLaren for the 1980 season that was vetoed by the board. When Neerpasch left to join Talbot a year later, he announced that he would be taking the engine with him.

Dieter Stappert, who took over from

LEFT Paul Rosche oversaw the complete development of the M12/13 engine from its road car routes to F1 title. *(John Townsend)*

PAUL ROSCHE – BMW MOTORSPORT

Paul Rosche joined BMW in 1957 and remained there for the rest of his career. During that time he was responsible for a host of high-performance engines and their racing counterparts, the most famous of which was the M12/13 that powered Nelson Piquet to the 1983 World Championship title.

After the Formula 1 project ended, Rosche continued his relationship with Gordon Murray by designing the 6.1-litre V12 used in the McLaren F1 road car, while success on track continued in the shape of the Le Mans programme that took place in conjunction with Williams.

He oversaw the conceptualisation of the V10 engine that took BMW back to Formula 1 before retiring in 1999.

LEFT Rosche and BMW had an aggressive development programme, constantly updating in pursuit of more power. *(John Townsend)*

Neerpasch, was determined to prevent this from happening. He told Henry: 'I found out that, although they had started talking and negotiating the contractual terms, there was not even as much as a letter of intent on the files. The engine wasn't built by this stage, so I tried to persuade the board not to sell it to Talbot. I wanted the company to keep the engine

design, develop it properly and find a partner with whom to enter grand prix racing.'

In April 1980 the board rubber-stamped the decision to build and supply the engine, and Stappert set about finding a partner. A deal with Brabham was agreed later that year.

Stappert explained the reasoning to Henry: 'First, it was clearly a well-financed, high-technology team. Secondly, Gordon Murray is one of the very best designers. Thirdly, Nelson Piquet is one of the very best drivers.'

During the winter of 1980/81, a test mule dubbed the BT49T was built. But Brabham stuck with its Cosworth-powered chassis for the 1981 season, and following a tense final race at Las Vegas Piquet claimed his first World Championship title and the first for Brabham in the Ecclestone era.

At the British Grand Prix at Silverstone that year, Piquet gave the BT50 its public début. The car shared the same monocoque as the BT49, but in the back was BMW's 1.5-litre turbo instead of the 3.0-litre Cosworth V8. The BT50 only ran during the opening free practice session and Piquet recorded a time of 1m 12.60s, which compared with his best of 1m 11.95s in the BT49C.

The BT50 was not seen again at a grand prix until the opening race of 1982 in South Africa. This was despite a trying winter test period through which the turbo-engine car was beset by reliability issues, while the atmospheric version was on song and flying.

Stappert told Henry: 'We were down there at Paul Ricard and Patrese had just been signed from Arrows. He was going round and round in the BT49C-Cosworth, setting new lap records all the time. But Nelson never once thought about getting into the Cosworth car even though there was one standing in the next garage. He wasn't interested. He was always optimistic about the turbo and never wavered in his support… even though at one point Paul Rosche and I felt like going down to Marseilles harbour, climbing aboard a sailing boat and vanishing for good!'

The race début of the Brabham-BMWs at Kyalami was hardly a star-studded affair as Piquet crashed out and Patrese succumbed to a turbo bearing failure. For the following races in Brazil and Long Beach, the Brabham drivers were entered in Cosworth-powered BT49Ds. Like the other FOCA teams, Brabham skipped the San Marino Grand Prix, a move that provoked a tersely worded statement from BMW.

'BMW has threatened to "terminate its co-operation" with the Brabham Formula 1 team if the two Brabham-BMW cars do not race at the Belgian Grand Prix at Zolder on May 9.

'The warning comes in a letter sent today to Mr Bernie Ecclestone, chief of the Brabham team and President of the Formula One Constructors' Association, whose members boycotted Sunday's San Marino Grand Prix in a row over minimum weight regulations.

'World Champion Nelson Piquet and team-mate Riccardo Patrese did not race their BMW

ABOVE The race debut for the M12/13 came at the 1982 South African GP, but neither car finished. *(LAT)*

LEFT Turbo bearing failure accounted for Patrese in South Africa, while Piquet crashed out of the BMW's race début. *(LAT)*

turbo engine Brabhams because of the boycott and the letter to Mr. Ecclestone demands "that Brabham adheres to the agreement between the two companies and races two Brabham-BMW cars in the Belgian Grand Prix", adding that should this requirement not be met by Mr. Ecclestone, BMW will terminate its co-operation with Brabham.'

Both Piquet and Patrese were back in the BT50s for the race at Zolder, where Piquet finished three laps down in fifth place and Patrese spun out. The Italian used the Cosworth-powered car for Monaco, where he scored one of the most remarkable wins in Formula 1 history, crossing the line to claim his maiden grand prix victory despite having spun a lap earlier.

Meanwhile, Piquet persevered with the BT50, and endured the indignity of failing to qualify in Detroit. As Saturday's session was a wash-out, the grid was settled in Friday qualifying, when Piquet suffered a blown engine and then had pick-up problems in the spare car.

Frustrations were mounting on both sides. BMW was demanding that Brabham run two turbo cars, while Brabham was becoming impatient with the extent of the reliability problems it was encountering.

BELOW Piquet leads the way in the 1982 Canadian GP – the first win for the Brabham-BMW combination.
(LAT)

Brabham's first turbo win

Tension with BMW threatened to boil over ahead of the Canadian Grand Prix at Montréal, but Brabham team manager Herbie Blash managed somehow to keep the peace. His diplomatic skills were tested even further when Piquet's car developed a misfire in free practice, but the Brazilian jumped into the spare car and it went on to run faultlessly, allowing him to take BMW's first-ever Formula 1 win.

Murray told Henry just how significant that moment was: 'Those early days with the turbo were like the Brabham-Alfa nightmares – only worse. The lowest point was Detroit, of course, where I honestly began to think we were banging our heads against a brick wall. But BMW made what was really a very simple alteration to the mixture control and it was transformed. I just can't over-emphasise the importance of that change: it went from totally undriveable, in Nelson's view, to behaving just like a Cosworth DFV. It was very nearly the end of the road for the whole deal and such a big decision was hanging on such a minor alteration to the engine.'

Piquet also finished second next time out

at Zandvoort, but thereafter the 1982 season's only other top-six finishes for the BT50 were fourth and fifth places for Piquet and Patrese in the Swiss Grand Prix at Dijon. However, the success in Montréal had proved that the engine could be a winner, and there was the prospect of even more power to come.

New thinking for the BT52

The promise of all this extra horsepower from BMW was the driving force behind the design philosophy of the BT52, as Murray explains.

'Because the BMW engine should have had a power advantage and, knowing Paul Rosche, would have more and more power as the season developed, I thought I would just have to develop the weight distribution.

'I knew I wasn't going to have time to do all the wind-tunnel testing, so I dumped the sidepods and just went for downforce from conventional wings, which is very "draggy" relative to ground effect, but I really had no choice. So, that's why it's that arrow shape.

'Everything is at the back. I had no idea – I didn't even have time to do crude calculations – but I knew once we lost downforce we were going to be traction-limited out of second- and third-gear corners.

'All Formula 1 cars were traction-limited out of hairpins at Monaco, because the downforce is hardly working, but once you are doing 80–100mph the downforce helps so much on the traction. During the ground-effect years all of us – all the designers – slowly but surely moved the weight distribution and the centre of pressure more and more forwards because

you didn't need it on the back for traction. And we ended up with cars getting towards 50/50 weight distribution, which was unheard of in Formula 1.

'So I knew that was going to take a dive and we wouldn't have any traction! So on the drawing board I just pushed everything, every item I could possibly find, to the back of the car, and adjusted the wheelbase to get – from memory – seven per cent weight shift to the back axle from the 50/50.

'It was a huge risk. I didn't know if that was too much or not enough. If it wasn't enough, too bad – because there was nothing else I could

move to the back. The front had nothing in it – basically just the monocoque and the driver's legs. So that was the sort of starting point.'

There was another significant area of new thinking in the BT52. The new car was designed with a fuel tank of just 42 gallons – committing Brabham to making a refuelling pit-stop in each race.

At the 1982 British Grand Prix at Brands Hatch, the BT50s appeared with two quick-release couplings on their fuel tanks. The reason was clear – Brabham was preparing to pit the cars for mid-race refuelling. This concept was far from new: cars had always pitted to top up fuel in the old days of Formula 1, refuelling was normal in endurance sports-car racing such as at the Le Mans 24 Hours, and it featured in the Indianapolis 500. It was a visit to Indy that convinced Murray the concept could work in Formula 1.

'From the testing we'd done at Donington on pit-stops, we had a bogey time of about 26 seconds. So if we didn't lose any more than 26 seconds in the pits, we were going to win the race.

'It was just mathematics. It's a very easy calculation – you don't need to be a mathematician. On the same tyres, on the same day and with the same track conditions, for every pound (0.5kg) you took out of the car it went a hundredth of a second a lap quicker. It was pretty linear actually. And you knew that because you practised the car empty and you practised the car full on the same tyres.

'That bit was very easy, but also I knew that the tyres peaked on lap three or four and then slowly but surely, depending on track conditions, they degraded and that off-set the speed you gained by losing the weight of the fuel during the race. You had the weight decrease having a pretty linear performance increase and then you had the tyre graph overlaid over that dropping off over the race. And I thought if you could put new tyres on at a point in the race and you could carry less weight… that's a pit-stop.'

The Brabhams lined up second and third at Brands Hatch in 1982, with Patrese ahead. This became pole when Keke Rosberg's Williams stalled on the dummy grid, but Patrese then stalled at the actual start, leaving Piquet to sprint away into the lead. But before the Brazilian had a chance to establish the magic

DAVID NORTH – DESIGNER

David North gave up a career in the civil service to follow his love of cars and work in Formula 1. His CV landed on Gordon Murray's desk just as Brabham was seeking to expand its design department in 1979. In a team of just two, North was responsible for a large part of the design work on the Brabhams of that era, especially the transmissions, aero and engine installation.

He followed Murray to McLaren, where he headed up the transmission department. From there he moved to the Renault/Benetton/Lotus team, where he again specialised in transmissions. He was working as Head of Advance Projects until he retired in 2014.

LEFT David North (left), Alastair Caldwell and Nelson Piquet. *(John Townsend)*

26-second lead, the car ground to a halt after a fuel metering unit drive pulley came loose.

Patrese again out-qualified Piquet as the Brabhams started fourth and sixth for the French Grand Prix at Paul Ricard. Once the race was underway, their weight advantage came to the fore and in just five laps they were running first and second, with the Italian ahead. An engine blow-up brought Patrese's race to a fiery end on lap eight, while Piquet's race was concluded by another, less spectacular engine failure.

Piquet was the faster of the two as they lined up third and fifth for the German Grand Prix and the Brazilian wasted no time in getting to the front, passing Renault's René Arnoux to lead on lap two. Piquet romped away and was 24 seconds ahead when he came up to lap the ATS of Eliseo Salazar on lap 24. Not wishing to lose a precious second, Piquet made an impatient and ill-judged move on the Chilean as they entered the first chicane. There was contact and both cars were eliminated. Piquet was furious and the punches and kicks he aimed at Salazar as they squared up in the gravel trap become one of sport's most (in) famous live televised moments. Patrese, almost inevitably, was sidelined by a blown engine.

Next time out in Austria, however, Patrese's engine held together long enough for the Brabham to pit from the lead as planned. A

stop of 15.6 seconds meant that the Italian resumed the race in front. For three glorious laps he carried on at the head of the field, but any hopes of a second career win ended when a gudgeon pin broke and the engine seized, sending him spinning out of the race. Piquet, who had pitted early after blistering his tyres, had his race brought to a premature conclusion by a broken camshaft.

Returning to the BT52's design, the smaller fuel tank also gave further scope for Murray to work on the packaging at the rear of the car.

'Behind the front axle centre line, you've got driver, fuel tank and engine and transmission, and the chances of moving mass around with a full-tank car is virtually impossible,' he explains. 'You can move the battery or the radiators – half a per cent, maybe one per cent. Once you go to a shorter fuel tank you can actually choose an engine spacer or a bellhousing spacer or a longer gearbox and you can shift the weight massively. That's how I managed to get so many things so far back.

'Because I got rid of the sidepods, I had to fit the radiator and the intercoolers somewhere and David North and I worked on that shape. It just came out of the shape of the intercooler and radiator. And it happened to look nice too. My theory has always been why make a racing car ugly if what you're doing doesn't affect the aerodynamics?'

ABOVE An all-too familiar feeling for Patrese as an engine blows during the 1982 Italian GP at Monza. *(John Townsend)*

Chapter Three

The BT52 in action

Turbos dominated the 1983 Formula 1 season, Brabham, Ferrari and Renault each winning four races. But it was the BMW-powered BT52 – a light, small and fabulously attractive dart-shaped design – that sprung the big surprises of a season in which Renault's Alain Prost was hot favourite. The BT52 won first time out, for Nelson Piquet at home in Brazil, and then a late-season charge saw Brabham also win the last three races, with Piquet's results – two firsts and a third – allowing him to snatch the World Championship title from Prost by two points.

OPPOSITE Piquet was fourth in Detroit, the leading turbo car as the Cosworths enjoyed a last hurrah. *(John Townsend)*

ABOVE First ever run for the BT52 took place in secrecy at Brands Hatch. *(LAT)*

Heavily disguised, and under maximum security, the BT52 hit the track at Brands Hatch in early March 1983 for a shakedown with Piquet at the wheel. The car was officially launched at BMW's Munich headquarters a few days later before being flown out to Brazil, where it took part in pre-race testing in Rio ahead of the season's opening round there.

Remarkably, the team had three of the new chassis ready for testing in Rio. Piquet instantly demonstrated the car's potential by recording the fastest time during the first morning, before a gearbox issue intervened. Patrese drove on the second day of testing until halted by an engine problem, something that would be a recurring theme for him that season. Piquet was again second fastest on the third and final day, when he put some mileage on the spare car.

This is how the times looked after the BT52's first official test session:

1	Derek Warwick	Toleman-Hart TG183B	1m 35.17s
2	Nelson Piquet	Brabham-BMW BT52	1m 35.37s
3	Andrea de Cesaris	Alfa Romeo 183T	1m 35.68s
4	Niki Lauda	McLaren-Cosworth MP4/1C	1m 35.90s
5	Riccardo Patrese	Brabham-BMW BT52	1m 36.26s
6	Jean-Pierre Jarier	Ligier-Cosworth JS21	1m 36.63s

RIGHT Patrese puts some miles on the BT52 in pre-season testing at Rio. *(LAT)*

The new Brabham was the talk of the paddock in testing, and not just because of the times it set despite very little previous running. Murray's sidepod-free design resulted in a sleek-looking car with a narrow, pointed nose, a distinctive and unique delta-shaped front wing, and a thin, dart-like body – all topped off by a huge rear wing. The car was tiny in comparison with its rivals, which – with the exception of Ligier – kept faith with longer sidepods despite the 'skirtless' rules.

The pretty-looking car, with its small fuel tank, had been designed and built in record time. It had gone well in testing, but the true level of its competitiveness would only become apparent when it raced. At the Brazilian Grand Prix on 13 March 1983, this question would be answered.

Brazilian GP, Jacarepagua
13 March 1983

Brabham's all-new BT52 had shown well during its only official pre-season test, but testing can

LEFT Testing had gone well, but the team wasn't confident going into the race. *(LAT)*

be a fickle business from which it is notoriously difficult to draw conclusions. It is only in the white heat of battle that teams are forced to show their true level of competitiveness and thus Brabham went into the season-opening race at Rio in Brazil unsure of exactly what to expect.

The tight rear packaging of the car initially caused some problems during the opening practice session, with the heat from the turbo particularly affecting the gearbox and the left-rear damper. As a result the team opted to keep the turbo boost pressure down, while overnight a new cooling duct was added to the left-hand rear bodywork.

Piquet was fifth fastest in the first official qualifying session, with Patrese sixth. It was even hotter for the Saturday qualifying session, but with the additional cooling in place Piquet was able to set the fourth best time, recording a lap at 1m 35.114s compared with the 1m 34.526s set by Keke Rosberg to take pole position for Williams. This would be the last-ever pole for the Cosworth DFV, and the last for a normally aspirated engine until turbos were outlawed for the 1989 season.

ABOVE Piquet worked his way past Rosberg to take the lead of his home race. *(Foto Ercole Colombo)*

RIGHT The huge crowd was delighted by Piquet's performance in Brazil. *(LAT)*

Piquet built up a huge lead and was able to back off and preserve the engine.
(John Townsend)

Patrese was back in seventh with 1m 35.958s but, like Piquet, he made a great start and the Brabhams were third and fourth as they exited the first corner of the opening lap. Like Brabham, Williams had chosen to make a mid-race refuelling stop, and Rosberg, running light, sprinted off into an early lead.

On lap two Piquet lined up Alain Prost down the back straight and outbraked the Renault into the hairpin. The Brazilian then set the fastest lap of the race as he reeled in Rosberg for the lead. Meanwhile, Patrese had also passed Prost. The BT52 was making an impressive début.

With Rosberg suffering with tyre graining, Piquet had little difficulty in taking the lead on lap seven to the audible delight of the 70,000-strong crowd. Once ahead Piquet quickly established a comfortable lead, easily building up an advantage bigger than Murray's magic 26 seconds long before he was due to make his refuelling stop.

Patrese had pitted though, but this was an unscheduled stop. The Italian was right on the back of Rosberg when a broken exhaust sapped the power from his BMW engine. His tyres were changed and he was sent back out, but he was back in to retire a lap later.

Rosberg pitted earlier than intended, on lap 29, as a result of his tyre degradation. The stop was a dramatic one, with a flash fire erupting during the refuelling process. The Finn jumped from his car as the flames were extinguished and then hopped back in. Williams push-started the car to get him going again, but this was an infringement of the rules and he was later struck from the race results.

Piquet pitted for his fuel and tyres as planned on lap 40. The stop went smoothly, although the Brazilian was slightly slow in getting away. The whole process took 16.9 seconds and he rejoined with a lead of almost a minute. His advantage would have been less if John Watson had not retired a little earlier from second place when his McLaren's Cosworth engine seized.

Under no pressure, Piquet stroked the car home. Rosberg fought his way back into second place and brought the gap down to under 30 seconds, but the result was never in doubt.

'It was easy,' Piquet said after the race. 'I didn't even have the normal boost on the turbo.'

'The car was falling apart at the end of the race but we didn't know that at the time!' reveals Charlie Whiting, the team's chief mechanic. 'The intercooler was broken, the exhausts were all broken, and it probably wouldn't have hung on for an awful lot longer. Although pre-season testing was good, we weren't confident that we were going to win. But Nelson did a brilliant job there, as he always did in Rio. It was amazing.'

BELOW FISA President Jean-Marie Balestre congratulates race-winner Piquet.
(Foto Ercole Colombo)

US GP, Long Beach
27 March 1983

Although the streets of Long Beach, home to round two of the 1983 World Championship, were the scene of Piquet's first Formula 1 win, in 1980, the US Grand Prix West was a much less happy hunting ground for the Brazilian this time around.

In qualifying Piquet was unhappy with the grip from his Michelin tyres and lined up a disappointing 20th, almost four seconds down on the pole-setting pace of Ferrari's Patrick Tambay. Patrese fared better in 11th spot, but was still 2.8 seconds off Tambay.

Once again Patrese made a stellar start and was up to seventh place by the end of the first lap. He put a nice move on Tyrrell's Danny Sullivan and soon caught the pack ahead, making it a six-way fight for the lead.

He became briefly detached from the group as he struggled to pass the troubled Ferrari of René Arnoux. Once ahead he again closed on the lead group, which was headed by the duelling Tambay and Rosberg. A charging Jean-Pierre Jarier briefly demoted Patrese back to fifth, but when the Ligier driver tangled with Michele Alboreto as they disputed fourth, Patrese was able to nip by the pair of them.

Fourth became second when Tambay and Rosberg collided. This left the second Williams of Jacques Laffite in the lead, with Patrese tucked in behind him. However, behind them the McLarens of John Watson and Niki Lauda were closing in. Patrese tried to force the issue and make a move for the lead but outbraked himself and went off. He joined in fourth place behind the two McLarens.

Patrese finally pulled a successful move on Laffite, who had been passed by both McLarens. Third place was in the bag for the Brabham driver only for the distributor to break just three laps from home. It is worth

noting that Patrese had completed all these laps on a single tank of fuel, the team having decided that the layout of the pitlane at Long Beach would have made refuelling too time-consuming. As would become evident later in the season at the other street circuits on the calendar, Monaco and Detroit, the BT52 could last a race distance without refuelling if turbo boost pressure was reduced.

It was a race to forget for Piquet. From 20th on the grid, a sluggish start dropped him even further back. He started to work his way up the order but lack of grip and a sticking throttle hampered him. He had broken into the top ten when the throttle finally stuck for good and he carried on straight down an escape road and into retirement.

From the highs of Brazil, this was a rude awakening for the Brazilian but he was still second in the championship and there was three weeks before round three, the French Grand Prix at Paul Ricard.

ABOVE The bumpy track surface gave Patrese a rough ride at Long Beach.
(John Townsend)

LEFT Piquet fights with 1980 F1 World Champion Alan Jones, making his only F1 start for Arrows.
(John Townsend)

The last-ever non-championship Formula 1 race took place at Brands Hatch on 10 April 1983. As the Race of Champions clashed with a major Group C sports-car race at Monza (where Riccardo Patrese was driving for the works Lancia team) and a key Michelin tyre test at Paul Ricard (where Nelson Piquet was a participant), Brabham asked Mexican driver Hector Rebaque to step in.

Rebaque entered 58 grands prix between 1977 and 1981 for Hesketh and Brabham as well as his own eponymous team. He raced for Brabham for part of the 1980 season and the whole of 1981, but then failed to find a Formula 1 drive for 1982 and accepted an offer to race in CART in the US.

Rebaque's BT52 was one of just 13 cars entered for the Race of Champions, but a significant presence was Stefan Johansson's Spirit-Honda, in which the Japanese firm's V6 turbo Formula 1 engine was making its race début.

'It's a long story,' Rebaque says of his one-off drive. 'I finished the relationship with Bernie in 1981 when Parmalat wanted an Italian driver. At that moment he called and told me to wait until he could figure out how not to have an Italian driver. But it was too late for me to go to another team, so I decided to retire.

'While I was retired from racing I was invited to race Indycars and I think I did six races, but it wasn't really what I wanted to do. Then Bernie came back to me with the idea of having a third Brabham with a Ford turbo. The intention was to make the car for 1983 but this kept on getting delayed, so by the time the Race of Champions came Bernie said, "Why don't you come and drive the car otherwise by the time they finish the engine you'll be completely out of shape".'

This offer came on the Friday a week before the race. Rebaque was back in Mexico City at the time. He jumped on a plane and headed to

BELOW Rebaque never got to grips with the handling of the BT52 and eventually pulled out of the race. *(Martin Lee)*

Brands Hatch, but there was no time to test or do any real pre-race preparation.

He struggled to get to grips with the BT52 and the BMW turbo engine. He qualified tenth, 3.8 seconds off the pole position time set by Keke Rosberg's Williams-Cosworth.

Things did not go much better in the race. Unhappy with the handling of the car, Rebaque made an unscheduled pit-stop for a fresh set of tyres, but when this failed to improve the balance he retired, citing tyre and suspension problems.

'I hadn't driven in Formula 1 for a year and a half,' says Rebaque. 'Some testing would have helped. I found the car very difficult to drive. We made a few changes and I think we got a little bit lost on the set-up and it got worse and worse. And that was a shame because it was great for me to be there with the Brabham team.'

Rebaque did have some prior experience of the BMW turbo, having had a role in the development of the BT50 during the 1981 season. Indeed, the Mexican could have played a more significant part in the history of the combination had the decision to enter him in the 1981 Italian Grand Prix in the turbo car not been overturned.

'During 1981 I'd been at all the testing sessions where we'd developed the BMW engine,' he says. 'There was an idea to race the BMW turbo at Monza in 1981 and the plan was that I would drive the car. But the championship was very tight for Nelson and the team was worried that it would be very difficult for the car to finish the race, so at the end of the day the decision was taken that we would go with two Cosworth cars in order to have more chances of taking points.'

After the outing at Brands Hatch, Rebaque returned to Mexico and waited for Bernie to call about the Brabham-Ford plan. But after six weeks or so of waiting, the call that finally came was to inform him that the project was dead. Rebaque believes that the engine never reached expectations on the dyno and therefore the project was canned.

With this disappointment, Rebaque decided to retire again, and this time it was for good. Since then he has concentrated on running a successful architecture business in his native Mexico City.

'I didn't want to drive anything else,' he said. 'Even though I went to drive Indy and won a race, it wasn't really for me. So I decided that if I wasn't going to have a ride in Formula 1 I'd go and do something else. I was still very young. I retired at 26 – I could have raced for another ten years, but it didn't happen.'

Despite the small entry, the Race of Champions was an exciting encounter. René Arnoux stormed into an early lead in his Ferrari but, according to Denis Jenkinson's *Motor Sport* report of the race, this resulted in him wearing out his tyres. This allowed Rosberg to take over the lead, and the Williams driver built a commanding advantage before he too was slowed by tyre wear. In the closing laps Danny Sullivan moved his Tyrrell onto the tail of the Williams, but could not find a way by, eventually falling just half a second short in a thrilling conclusion to an era.

LEFT Rebaque retired from racing after the Race of Champions aged just 26.
(John Townsend)

ABOVE **Piquet battled his way to second in the revised BT52 at the French GP.**
(John Townsend)

French GP, Paul Ricard
17 April 1983

The three Brabham BT52s arrived in southern France with a series of updates. The engine cover and wings were revised, the final drive was upgraded, and – perhaps most significantly – the car was now fitted with three onboard air jacks designed to save precious seconds in pit-stops. One jack was located at the front of the car around the bulkhead, while the other two were on either side at the rear underneath the short sidepods.

A turbo failure forced Piquet into the spare car for Friday qualifying. Although he was unhappy with its handling, he was still able to set the fourth fastest time. The handling issues remained for Saturday, but that was the least of the Brazilian's worries. In final practice a broken exhaust allowed hot air to escape on to the rear wing mounts, causing them to fail and the wing to fly off!

Patrese had more luck and was able to improve his Friday time in order to line up third, while Piquet slipped back to sixth. Again the Italian made a good start to sprint into second place, while Piquet bravely squeezed by Arnoux to take fourth.

Prost was in a class of his own out front, and Eddie Cheever soon made it a Renault 1–2 as he overtook Patrese. Piquet was the next driver to pass Patrese and he soon set about chasing down Cheever, taking second from the American on lap 18. Not long after Patrese brought his car into the pits to retire, its engine having lost all coolant.

When Prost stalled in the pits after stopping for a fresh set of Michelin tyres and – for the first time at Renault – a top-up of fuel, Piquet took over the lead. On lap 32 the Brabham driver put the new hydraulic jacks to the test when he came in for his scheduled stop. They worked perfectly and he was on his way in 16.1

RIGHT **A loss of engine coolant ended Patrese's race at Paul Ricard.**
(John Townsend)

seconds, with Prost back in the lead but Piquet now ahead of Cheever in second place.

Prost controlled the race from the front to take a comfortable win, and while Piquet was never happy with the balance of his car he finished well ahead of Cheever. His six points put him clear at the top of the standings, but Prost and Renault had demonstrated that they would be a force to be reckoned with.

San Marino GP, Imola
30 April 1983

The Brabham drivers duelled with the Ferraris and Renaults for pole position for the San Marino Grand Prix, with Arnoux eventually prevailing for Ferrari. Piquet sat alongside him on the front row, while Patrese lined up fifth.

An engine problem in the warm-up forced Piquet into the spare car for the race, which started disastrously for the Brazilian as he stalled on the grid. Amazingly everybody managed to avoid him and he was push-started by the marshals.

Patrese, in contrast, made yet another good start and was running third behind the Ferraris of Arnoux and Tambay. Much to the consternation of the crowd, Patrese made short work of the red cars, outbraking Arnoux for the lead on lap four.

In the gap between Long Beach and Paul Ricard, a number of teams added refuelling valves to their cars. One of these was Ferrari, who had successfully put the refuelling routine to the test in the French Grand Prix and intended to repeat it at Imola. This meant that while Patrese was 'only' six seconds ahead of Tambay, the Frenchman would be pitting too, and so the 'magic' 26-second advantage no longer applied.

But Patrese over-shot his marks when he came into the pits, causing one of the air guns to become disconnected as the mechanic stretched to make it reach. All of his advantage was lost and his stop took 23.3 seconds compared with just 15 for Tambay's.

Piquet had fought his way into the top six by the time he made his scheduled stop. Nailing the pitlane markers, the Brabham team turned him around in just over 11 seconds. But it was to be in vain as a broken valve in the engine ended his charge soon after.

But Patrese upheld team honour in the later stages and closed right up on Tambay, taking the lead into Tamburello as a misfire slowed the Ferrari. But in his desire to pull out a lead, Patrese made a mistake at Acque Minerali and slid off the road, crashing into the tyre barriers. His fastest lap was scant consolation for a result that could have thrown him into the fight for the championship, which Piquet now led jointly with Prost.

BELOW Piquet stalled at the start in San Marino and was then halted by a broken valve. *(John Townsend)*

LEFT In Monaco, Piquet was one of the first to pit for slicks and was rewarded with second place. *(John Townsend)*

Monaco GP, Monte Carlo
15 May 1983

The tight confines of the Monaco paddock meant the race organisers issued a pre-race edict limiting the amount of fuel that could be stored in each garage to just 50 litres per car. This effectively ruled out mid-race refuelling and left Brabham, with its under-sized fuel tank, having to run with reduced boost to make the end of the race.

With Saturday qualifying washed out, the grid was decided by the times from the Friday session. This was bad news for Patrese, who had his Friday session cut short after the air-collector box from the fuel injection system fell off, bringing the car to a halt. With no chance to improve, he had to start from 17th, while Piquet lined up sixth.

There was further rain on race day and Piquet and Patrese, like all the other drivers bar Rosberg, started on grooved rain tyres. Rosberg's call was sublime as the track was drying and from fifth on the grid he was in the lead before the end of the lap. Piquet made a slow getaway and dropped to ninth, but was one of the first to change tyres, pitting for slicks on lap four.

When the rest followed suit Piquet was up to sixth, which became fifth when he passed Prost going through the tunnel. Fifth became third when Marc Surer and Derek Warwick collided at Ste Devote as they battled over the final podium place. When Jacques Laffite pitted to retire his Williams, Piquet became second.

A year on from his maiden Formula 1 win, Patrese was in inspired form and was promoted to fourth by Laffite's retirement. But the Italian was running low on fuel and needed to make a late 'splash-and-dash' to ensure he made the finish. Just after he rejoined, the fuel injection system failed and his spirited drive was over.

RIGHT Patrese was in great form, but his strong drive ended in retirement. *(John Townsend)*

LEFT Flames lick from the back of Patrese's BMW engine as the Italian fights his way up the order. *(John Townsend)*

Second place meant that Piquet now had a two-point lead over Prost, who followed the Brabham home in third place.

Belgian GP, Spa-Francorchamps
22 May 1983

The 1983 Belgian Grand Prix marked the return of the Spa-Francorchamps circuit to the Formula 1 calendar, albeit in abridged 4.33-mile form. As was the case in Monaco, rain during Saturday's qualifying session meant that Friday times set the grid. Piquet started fourth despite not being particularly happy with the handling of his BT52, while Patrese lined up directly behind him in sixth position.

With the initial start aborted, the race began at the second time of asking. Piquet made a good start, but was baulked going into the first corner and lost a place to Arnoux, dropping to fifth. Patrese slotted into sixth, but on the run to Les Combes his BMW engine let go in spectacular fashion and he coasted to a halt in a ball of smoke.

While Andrea de Cesaris was surprisingly setting the pace for Alfa Romeo, Piquet was putting Arnoux under pressure, finally taking fourth place from the Frenchman on lap 18. This became third when de Cesaris pitted for a fresh set of tyres, a stop that took longer than it should have done.

A quicker pit-stop moved Piquet ahead of

Tambay and into second, but with Prost almost half a minute up the road victory seemed out of reach. This was reinforced in the closing stages when Piquet lost the use of fifth gear. This dropped him into the clutches of Tambay and Cheever, who demoted him to fourth.

With Prost claiming his second win of the year, Piquet dropped to second in the championship, four points adrift of the Renault driver.

ABOVE Piquet charged his way into second place in the Belgian GP at Spa... *(John Townsend)*

LEFT ...only for the car to become stuck in fifth gear, dropping him back to fourth place. *(John Townsend)*

United States GP, Detroit
5 June 1983

Formula 1 headed back to the United States for round seven, which was held on the streets of Detroit. Piquet had a strong qualifying and lined up on the front row next to pole-sitter Arnoux in the Ferrari. Patrese was forced into the spare after his race car developed a fuel leak and after failing to find a clear lap during qualifying he started back in 15th position.

When de Cesaris stalled his Alfa Romeo the first start was aborted, but at the second time of asking Piquet made a flier to take the lead from Arnoux. The lead pair quickly established a comfortable gap over the rest, but Piquet was coming under increasing pressure from the Frenchman.

The Ferrari was soon close enough to make a move for the lead, but Piquet barely mustered any defence. Pre-race the Brabham team had decided not to make a fuel stop and instead Piquet was running with reduced boost in an effort to eke out his fuel for the full 60 laps.

Ferrari on the other hand was committed to bringing Arnoux in for a top-up, but all of this became academic when the fuel injection failed

ABOVE Piquet relaxes on the grid ahead of the challenging race at Detroit that lies ahead. *(John Townsend)*

RIGHT Piquet would eventually finish fourth in Detroit, after surrendering the lead due to a puncture. *(John Townsend)*

LEFT Patrese fights with the Ferrari of Patrick Tambay but gearbox problems ended his podium hopes. *(John Townsend)*

on his car and he coasted to a halt. Patrese's race was already over by this point, the brakes on his BT52 having given up the ghost.

Piquet, on his economy run, was now in the lead as the action took place behind him. By the closing stages Michele Alboreto had worked his Tyrrell-Cosworth into second place and was closing in. Piquet used the power of the turbo to keep the Italian at bay down the straight. But on lap 50 Piquet slowed – his left-rear tyre punctured.

He limped back to the pits for a new set of Michelins. He was also given a splash of fuel and was on his way again. But first place had become fourth as Alboreto romped home to claim the final win for the Cosworth DFV engine and the Tyrrell team.

Prost had been in subdued form all weekend and came home outside the points in eighth place, which meant that Piquet closed the gap in the championship back to a single point.

Canadian GP, Circuit Gilles Villeneuve
12 June 1983

Just five days after Detroit the Formula 1 teams were in action again in Montréal. Despite the short gap between races, Brabham introduced some minor aerodynamic changes to the BT52. Both drivers needed to take to the spare car during practice as Piquet experienced throttle problems and Patrese had an 'off' in the damp conditions, damaging the left-hand side of his intended race chassis.

In one of the closest qualifying sessions of the year, Piquet missed out on pole by just over

a tenth of a second, yet started third behind Arnoux and Prost. Patrese was seven-tenths further back in fifth position, having taken to the spare yet again following an engine failure in his race car.

Piquet made a slow getaway and was instantly passed by Patrese, who sprinted off the line to hold third place going into the first corner. The Italian was on a charge and passed Prost into the final corner to secure second.

Arnoux was clear in front with Patrese giving chase. Piquet passed Prost for third and the Renault driver struggled with a down-on-power engine. Piquet then reeled in his team-mate but before he could make a move he was touring into the pits to retire with a broken throttle cable.

BELOW A broken throttle cable prevented Piquet from taking back-to-back Canadian GP wins. *(John Townsend)*

LEFT Neither Brabham driver made it to the finish in the 1983 Canadian GP. *(John Townsend)*

Patrese upheld Brabham honour, briefly leading as Arnoux made his scheduled stop. When Patrese pitted soon after, the Brabham team turned him around in just 11.08 seconds, and he set off in renewed pursuit of the Ferrari.

But rather than challenge the Frenchman, Patrese was instead losing places, dropping behind Cheever and Tambay in quick succession as his car developed a gearbox problem, which eventually forced him out of the race.

Prost salvaged fifth place despite his difficulties, and extended his lead over Piquet in the championship to three points as the season reached its halfway stage. Tambay's third place meant that he was now level on points with the Brazilian.

British GP, Silverstone
16 July 1983

The Swiss Grand Prix was supposed to have been next up, but was cancelled due to the lack of a television deal. Thus there was over a month between races, allowing all the teams to test and make updates to their cars. Brabham duly arrived at Silverstone for the British Grand Prix with three all-new BT52Bs.

The most obvious difference between the old and new cars was the livery, with the white and blue colours having been transposed after livery designer Peter Stevens had made the observation to Bernie Ecclestone that the car didn't look quite right on TV. Less superficially, the BT52B featured a host of small modifications that included a new, longer nose and changes centred around the engine installation and suspension geometry.

Patrese used the short nose to qualify fifth, but for final qualifying Piquet's car was fitted with the long nose and he ended up sixth, less than one-tenth behind. Patrese's car also received the long nose for the race.

The Italian once again made a stellar start to go wheel-to-wheel with Prost for third place on the run into Copse corner. Piquet held sixth,

RIGHT The all-new Brabham BT52B made its debut at the British GP at Silverstone. *(John Townsend)*

CENTRE The new, smoother nose and revised livery is very clear in this picture. *(John Townsend)*

which became fifth when Elio de Angelis's new Lotus-Renault expired.

The same fate befell Patrese soon after, a blown turbo ensuring his race ended in a cloud of white smoke. This promoted Piquet to fourth and the Brazilian was soon hunting down Arnoux for third. The Ferraris were in tyre trouble around the fast Silverstone circuit and Prost displaced Tambay from the lead.

Piquet worked his way by Arnoux and then Tambay to lead briefly when Prost made his scheduled stop. The Renault team turned him around in 14.65 seconds. When Piquet pitted soon after he was stationary for only 12.26 seconds. Prost's lead was now just over 17 seconds and despite Piquet's best efforts that is pretty much where it remained for the rest of the race.

Prost's third win of the season extended his championship advantage over Piquet to six points, while Tambay's third place kept him in the hunt just three points further adrift.

German GP, Hockenheim
7 August 1983
BMW's home race at Hockenheim was the scene for round ten of the season, but Piquet's weekend got off to an inauspicious start as he was disrupted by an electrical failure in his race car and then overheating problems in the spare during opening free practice.

The gremlins carried over into Friday qualifying, with a misfire again forcing him to take to the spare. With Saturday's qualifying

RIGHT Second place at Silverstone kept Piquet firmly in the fight for the championship. *(John Townsend)*

washed out, the Friday times set the grid and thus Piquet lined up fourth and Patrese eighth, with Ferrari once again locking out the front row.

Neither Brabham driver got away well, but Piquet was able to hold on to fourth while Patrese clung to eighth. Piquet passed de Cesaris's Alfa for third during the opening lap and moved into second when Tambay retired his Ferrari with engine failure.

Arnoux was well ahead by this point but when, with the pit-stops, Brabham turned Piquet around in 11.12 seconds compared with Ferrari's 13.08, the fight for the lead was on. Piquet reduced the gap to under five seconds before dropping back slightly in lapped traffic, but then his race came to a spectacular end as a cracked fuel filter caused a blazing fire at the rear of the car. He pulled over at the nearest fire marshal post, but despite their quick

intervention the chassis was destroyed, such was the size of the blaze.

Piquet's retirement promoted Patrese to third. His engine had felt tight ever since his pit-stop (a sublime effort below ten seconds) and, in view of his record thus far during the season, he was waiting for the inevitable seizure. But the car carried on running to the finish and he duly collected his first points of the season.

Prost struggled with a missing fifth gear for most of the race – a real problem on the long, fast Hockenheim circuit – and trailed home a distant fourth. But with Piquet's late retirement, the Frenchman's championship lead was now up to nine points – the equivalent of a race win.

Austrian GP, Österreichring
14 August 1983

One of the old BT52s was upgraded to B-spec for the Austrian Grand Prix, which took place just a week later. The spare would be in demand too, as Patrese suffered an engine blow in Friday practice while Piquet's race car was afflicted with a lack of turbo boost pressure.

The cars ran more smoothly in qualifying and Piquet started from fourth spot, with Patrese directly in his wheel tracks in sixth. Piquet made a flying start and briefly shot into second place, but was forced to back off and allow Arnoux to take the position into the first corner.

The Ferraris were running one and two while Piquet was battling with Prost for third, the pair banging wheels as the Renault briefly squeezed underneath the Brabham. Patrese was next in line in fifth, but was gradually losing touch with the lead quartet.

When the leaders came up to lap Jarier the order was reshuffled. Tambay was blocked, which allowed not only Arnoux to nip by and take the lead but also Piquet to make an opportunistic dive into second.

As Arnoux and Prost dived into the pits for their fuel stops, so Piquet came under pressure from Tambay, the Frenchman taking the lead before pitting for his scheduled stop. But he would not rejoin, low oil pressure forcing his Ferrari into retirement. A blown engine accounted for Patrese around this part of the race too.

Piquet pitted from the lead and a stop of just 10.2 seconds allowed him to rejoin ahead of Arnoux. He drove defensively as his tyres

came up to temperature and then started to pull away before feeling his engine start to tighten. After he turned down the boost to preserve the motor he dropped into the clutches of Arnoux and then Prost.

The two Frenchmen then staged a great duel for the lead, which was settled in favour of the Renault driver. Prost's fourth win of the season opened up his lead in the championship to 14 points with only four races remaining. If Piquet was going to win his second world title he was going to need a dramatic change of fortune.

Dutch GP, Zandvoort
28 August 1983

Piquet's title hopes were boosted by a raft of changes brought on board for the Dutch Grand Prix, held on the coastal track at Zandvoort. As well as reverting to a previous configuration of rear suspension settings, the BT52s also featured engine improvements in the form of a new water-spray system designed to lower intercooler temperature, a revised exhaust layout, a larger turbine in the turbo, and a different boost control valve in order to minimise turbo lag at lower speeds.

ABOVE Piquet took his first pole position of the season at Zandvoort and led away from the start. (John Townsend)

BELOW Piquet and Prost staged a great battle for the lead, as Piquet's commitment here shows. (John Townsend)

Having taken pole position, 0.7s clear of the Ferrari of Tambay, Piquet led from the start and opened up his advantage at roughly a second per lap. Prost, after working his way past Renault team-mate Cheever and Tambay, gradually began to close in on the leader. When Piquet started to slide around on his worn tyres, Prost was right on top of him. Even though all their rivals then pitted, Piquet and Prost stayed out and their battle for the lead continued.

On a couple of occasions Prost lined up a move, but Piquet defended and held on in front. Then came a controversial incident when, on lap 50, Prost got alongside down the start/finish straight. Piquet did not even try to defend the corner, but Prost, off-line, lost the back end under braking and, as he controlled the slide, he ran into Piquet, sending his rival crashing out of the race.

Prost initially appeared to have got away with it, but later that lap his car understeered off the track and into the tyre barrier.

These two retirements promoted Patrese to second place behind Arnoux's Ferrari, but a miserable day for Brabham was compounded when the Italian's engine lost boost pressure and he coasted to a halt with just two laps to go.

The result meant that Arnoux rose to second place in the championship table, eight points behind Prost. Piquet remained 14 points adrift and, with only three races to go, his title chances appeared to be hanging by a thread.

Italian GP, Monza
11 September 1983

BMW fitted its engines with a bigger turbo for the super-fast challenge of Monza, where round

13 of the season – the Italian Grand Prix – was
held. Patrese used the extra power to great
effect, scoring the second pole position of his
career and in the process becoming the first
Italian to take pole for his home race since
Alberto Ascari in 1953. Piquet lined up fourth as
Brabham created a Ferrari sandwich.

Patrese made a sensational start and
took a comfortable lead into the first corner,
while Piquet out-sprinted the two Ferraris to
make it a Brabham 1–2. The blue-and-white
cars were pulling well clear of the pack, but
Patrese's time at the front was fleeting. As
he came through the Parabolica to complete
lap two, a huge belch of white smoke
appeared from the back of his car and his
race was over.

Piquet quickly opened up a huge lead and
when the turbo failed on Prost's Renault he
blasted by to lap the car just as the Frenchman
coasted into retirement. Such was Piquet's lead
that he was able to retain it following his pit-
stop of 10.15 seconds.

Piquet's second win of the year coupled
with Prost's retirement reduced the Brazilian's
points deficit to five. Arnoux's second place at
Monza meant that he was now just two points
behind Prost, ensuring there would be a tight
three-way fight for the title during the final two
races.

'There are still two races to go and it's very
difficult, but there's still a chance because the
car is running very strongly at the front and I
hope we can do it,' Piquet said after the race.

CENTRE Piquet's second win of the season
revived his title challenge. *(John Townsend)*

RIGHT With two races to go, Piquet was now
only five points behind Prost. *(John Townsend)*

ABOVE Patrese makes a stunning start to grab the lead at Brands Hatch in front of a packed crowd. *(John Townsend)*

BELOW The new rear winglets were added to create even more rear downforce and traction. *(John Townsend)*

European GP, Brands Hatch
25 September 1983

With the proposed New York Grand Prix having been delayed until 1984 (it still has not happened) and a race at Caesar's Palace in Las Vegas cancelled due to lack of interest, Brands Hatch owner John Webb agreed a last-minute deal to organise a European Grand Prix.

A rain shower during the final ten minutes of qualifying prevented many of the top runners from having a final low-fuel run and allowed Elio de Angelis to claim the first pole for Lotus since 1978. Patrese lined up alongside him on the front row, while Piquet qualified fourth in the aggressive-looking Brabham with its new winglets adorning the rear wing in a bid to create more downforce.

Patrese rocketed off the line to take the lead as Piquet slotted in behind the second Lotus of Nigel Mansell and fended off the challenge from Cheever's Renault. Piquet made his move on Mansell for third place at Hawthorns on lap three.

RIGHT There was a fantastic crowd on hand at Brands Hatch for the European GP, despite the race only being arranged at the 11th hour.
(John Townsend)

Up front Patrese had his hands full defending from de Angelis. The Lotus driver was determined to get ahead and when he tried to force his way underneath his fellow countryman into Surtees he spun and took Patrese out. Piquet sailed through into the lead, while Patrese rejoined just ahead of Prost in second. De Angelis was now back in sixth, but his race came to a smoky end a couple of laps later.

Prost relieved Patrese of second place on the run into Paddock Hill Bend on lap 16. With Patrese's rear suspension having been deranged in his earlier tangle, he was unable to keep pace with the Renault, but equally Prost was unable to take much out of Piquet's lead, which was now around ten seconds.

Arnoux had been running in fifth place just behind Cheever, but his World Championship hopes took a hit on lap 20 when he made a mistake and spun at Surtees. Even though he kept the Ferrari engine running, the car was

ABOVE Patrese makes his mid-race refuelling stop in the European GP, but a stuck wheel wrecks his chances.
(John Townsend)

LEFT Victory at Brands Hatch was Piquet's third of the season and showed he and the team were in a rich vein of form.
(John Townsend

beached on the kerb and by the time it had been pushed back onto the track he was back in 19th place.

Patrese's hopes of a podium finish were scuppered by a sticking right wheel during the pit-stops, which meant the normally swift Brabham team took 25 seconds to refuel and re-tyre their man. Amazingly, lightning struck twice and a wheel gun failed when Piquet came in for his stop, which took almost 20 seconds as the team frantically found a spare.

With Renault having taken just 13.9 seconds to service Prost, Piquet's ten-second lead was considerably diminished. But the Brazilian simply picked up where he had left off and soon started to stretch out an advantage again. Piquet duly wrapped up his third win of the season, while Patrese's delayed stop and handling difficulties consigned him to seventh.

Piquet's second win on the bounce reduced Prost's points lead to two. Arnoux's failure to score all but removed him from the title race, which would be decided in the South African Grand Prix at Kyalami.

South African GP, Kyalami
15 October 1983
An engine failure in free practice was not the ideal start to the race weekend for Piquet,

but he put this behind him to set the second fastest time in first qualifying, behind the Ferrari of Tambay. Piquet improved his time in second qualifying but remained second, while Patrese qualified third, Arnoux fourth and Prost fifth.

Brabham deployed a bold strategy for the race, giving Piquet only enough fuel for 23 laps in a bid to tempt Prost and Arnoux to overstretch their cars as they gave chase. The strategy immediately paid off with Piquet sprinting off the line and into the lead, with Patrese dutifully slotting in behind in second place.

In his lighter-than-usual car, Piquet opened up a two-second lead on the first lap and there after built his lead by a second a lap. Arnoux was in trouble almost from the start and engine failure ended his challenge on lap ten.

Prost was beaten off the line by de Cesaris and he spent the opening laps trying to find a way around the Alfa. Meanwhile Piquet was driving beautifully out in front and had opened up a lead of over 20 seconds when he came in for his stop. The Brabham team had him off and running again in 11.67 seconds and he rejoined in the lead a few seconds ahead of Patrese, who had Niki Lauda's McLaren climbing all over him.

The TAG-badged Porsche turbo engine had

BELOW Light-fuelled, Piquet sprints away, leaving the pack in his wake at a second a lap at Kyalami.
(John Townsend)

RIGHT With Prost and Arnoux out, Piquet needed
to finish fourth or higher to win the title...
(John Townsend)

made its début mid-season and, in a portent
of what was to follow in 1984, Lauda was on a
charge at Kyalami. He had already passed de
Cesaris, Prost and Tambay, but the power of
the BMW turbo was making Patrese a tougher
nut to crack.

Piquet carried on where he had left off and
soon started to pull away again at a second
a lap. Just a couple of laps later Prost pitted.
But this was not his scheduled stop, and when
he unbuckled his belts and climbed from the
car following a drop in turbo pressure, the title
became Piquet's to lose.

Given the reliability problems the Brabham
team had experienced, it was no surprise that
Piquet, having been informed via pit board that
Prost was out, decided to turn down the boost
and ensure that he finished the race – he would
only be World Champion if he crossed the line
in fourth place or higher.

With Piquet cruising, Patrese soon caught
his team-mate and took over in the lead. A
few laps later and Lauda passed the Brazilian

for second place, but this was not to last as a
blown turbo ended the McLaren's race just four
laps from home.

By now only third-placed de Cesaris was on
the same lap as the Brabhams. Piquet backed
right off in the final laps to make sure of the
championship, allowing the Alfa driver to pass,
and his third place ensured that he secured his
second World Championship title by two points.
It had been an amazing turnaround over the last
four races.

BELOW ...so third
place was enough for
him and Brabham to
take their second title
in three seasons.
(John Townsend)

ABOVE First and third was a fitting way for Brabham to end a successful season. *(John Townsend)*

put less pressure on the turbocharger and I went and won the championship.'

The reason for Piquet's circumspection was understandable. On the first day of practice the team was in huge problems with premature detonation. To fix the issue, Paul Rosche and his team pulled the engines completely apart and rebuilt them in the back of a truck behind the pits. Amazingly, both engines held out in the race.

'Altitude was the problem,' Rosche states. 'The area around Johannesburg is about 1,800 metres and this caused a problem for the fuel injection. You have less air and you have to react. In Munich the altitude is about 500 metres. We went to South Africa and the day before the meeting we had a test. The engine was running well and then at the end of the test we turned up the boost to see for qualification. And the engine exploded!

'OK, we had enough engines, so we changed it. Then on the next day it was exactly the same: the engine was running well, we turned up the boost, and the engine exploded. That was a disaster as the next day was the race. What can we do? And that was the reason I opened the engine and looked inside – and I saw that it was running too lean. So I had to modify the injection to make the engine run richer. I just didn't know how much richer, I was thinking maybe five

'I had to finish fourth to win the championship,' Piquet recalls. 'We used 220 litres for a full race. And we started the race only with 70 litres. In the first six laps I was opening the gap at two seconds a lap, so I think they [Arnoux and Prost] got a little bit out of control, and they tried to put more power and they blew up.

'At that point I wanted to win the championship and I didn't care about Riccardo or anybody else. I had to finish in the top four and I saved the engine for most of the time. When Prost broke down I took my foot off and

RIGHT Piquet is about to spray the champagne once more as the post-season party kicks off. *(John Townsend)*

RIGHT With the party in full swing, Piquet is
prevented from giving a champagne soaking.
(John Townsend)

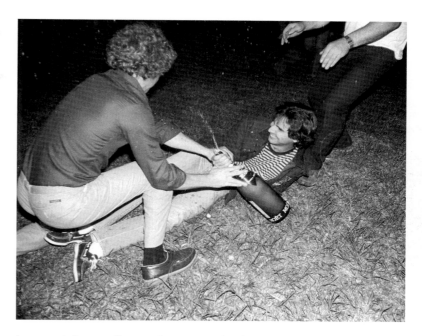

pe rcent or ten per cent, so in the end I went in the middle and decided on eight per cent. And then the engine was working perfectly and we had no problem.'

'We didn't have any agreement,' said Patrese, when asked if he and Piquet had discussed swapping positions before the race. 'It was the last race and it was really very important for him to finish in front of Prost because of the points. When Prost broke down Nelson just had to finish in the top four to have the points to overturn Prost in the championship.

'He was first and I was running second. I was following him and we were going a very conservative speed for maybe the last ten laps – and I didn't know what to do because there was no agreement. On the very long straight of Kyalami I saw that he was slowing down and I thought, "Oh my God, he's breaking down!" We were nearly stopping on the straight and then I went beside him and I looked at him and we tried to talk with our eyes! I was saying, "What's going on?" In the end he gave me a sign to go for the win and I overtook him.'

'The mood was amazing,' says Charlie Whiting. 'After Prost won in Austria, he was 14 points ahead. I remember seeing him leave the circuit surrounded by this entourage and it was almost like he was already World Champion – virtually a done deal. But it wasn't, so that was quite satisfying. We had the psychological advantage, big time.

'In South Africa I remember we were in a garage next to Renault and we were only separated by a fence, so we could see across to each other. We were having so much fun, playing music, doing exercises in the morning to limber up – things like this. It must have pissed them off. We were quite naughty and left bogus set-up sheets just within their view. It was quite amusing to watch them try to see these things without us seeing them. But everything written on them was rubbish.'

After the race, the whole team decamped to a ranch for a well-earned party to enjoy their success in appropriate style.

'That was quite a good party – I would say probably the best ever in my experience,' Whiting confesses. 'It was a proper party, and we had done something amazing. We were a small team and we celebrated as a team. Everyone was there – Nelson, Riccardo, the whole team. Bernie wasn't there though: he'd left and I think his parting shot to Herbie was to tell Piquet, "I pay him to win races not to come third!" I don't think he even saw Nelson after the race.'

BELOW The
celebrations went on
way into the small
hours of the morning!
(John Townsend)

Chapter Four

Anatomy of the BT52

The stunning and distinctive shape of the BT52 is a product of the length to which Gordon Murray and his team went to optimise the packaging in order to create a weight distribution biased as far to the rear as possible. In this chapter we'll look at how all the components came together to create a championship-winning package with a performance to match its looks.

OPPOSITE BT52 chassis 1 – fully restored by BMW Motorsport in 2013. *(Dirk Daniel Mann/BMW)*

RIGHT With the bodywork removed the simplicity of the BT52 front end is clear to see. (Dirk Daniel Mann/BMW)

BELOW The triangular object ahead of the steering wheel is the carbonfibre front rollover hoop. (Dirk Daniel Mann/BMW)

Chassis

As had become standard in Formula 1 by the 1980s, the chassis of the BT52 was a monocoque – the word is French and means 'single shell'. A monocoque is not only lighter than a traditional tubular spaceframe chassis, but also stronger, particularly with the developments that were taking place in composite technologies at the time of the BT52.

The origins of monocoque construction in racing car design go back to the Jaguar D-type, which used a 'semi-monocoque' structure in 1954, and the Lotus 25, which Colin Chapman developed in 1962 – and soon all Formula 1 cars were built around aluminium monocoques.

McLaren is widely credited with introducing carbonfibre to Formula 1 with the MP4/1 of 1981, but this car still had some metal components, including its roll hoop. The first all-carbon monocoque chassis was introduced by ATS on its D5, which Gustav Brunner designed for the 1983 season.

About 60 per cent of the BT52's monocoque chassis was carbonfibre, the rest being aluminium. The monocoque was built in two sections, the lower half from L72 aluminium panelling, the upper half from carbonfibre. It was the first new monocoque Brabham had designed since the BT48 of 1979, and it also featured the very first carbonfibre roll hoop, which gave the team some difficulties with the governing body, as Gordon Murray recalls.

'They said, "Hold on a minute, you have a plastic rollover bar." They said it should be tubular steel. If you look at the BT52 it has a very narrow front and I wanted to maximise

the airflow to the back wing. I had a tiny fuel tank that sits flat from end to end to try to get the air to the rear wing as cleanly as possible. Everybody else had big square tanks in front of the rear wing.

'It got to the point where I thought it was going to be stupid to put a metal hoop on top of that, so I just continued the carbonfibre up to a point and made a carbon rollover bar. I did all the stress calculations, and it had a tubular hole – like a toilet roll – in carbon bonded through it so you could pick up the car. The FIA went bananas. They said I couldn't do that. So just to really annoy them I made the little front rollover hoop in carbon as well. Normally most people just put a little steel or titanium thing there. The car passed the test.'

Rollover hoops aside, the chassis was fairly conventional, but what was attached to it was anything but. At both front and rear, Murray designed ground-breaking solutions that made the car incredibly simple to work on.

At the front this took the form of a cast magnesium structure that housed the upper wishbones, steering arms and the front air jack –

which made the scheduled pit-stops even faster.

'Because everything was at the back of the car – all the radiators, intercoolers, cooling – there was nothing in the nose, so I just wanted to make the smallest possible nose,' Murray explains. 'It had a very innovative front

RIGHT The cast magnesium block was designed by Murray to house the wishbones, steering arms, and springs and dampers. (Dirk Daniel Mann/BMW)

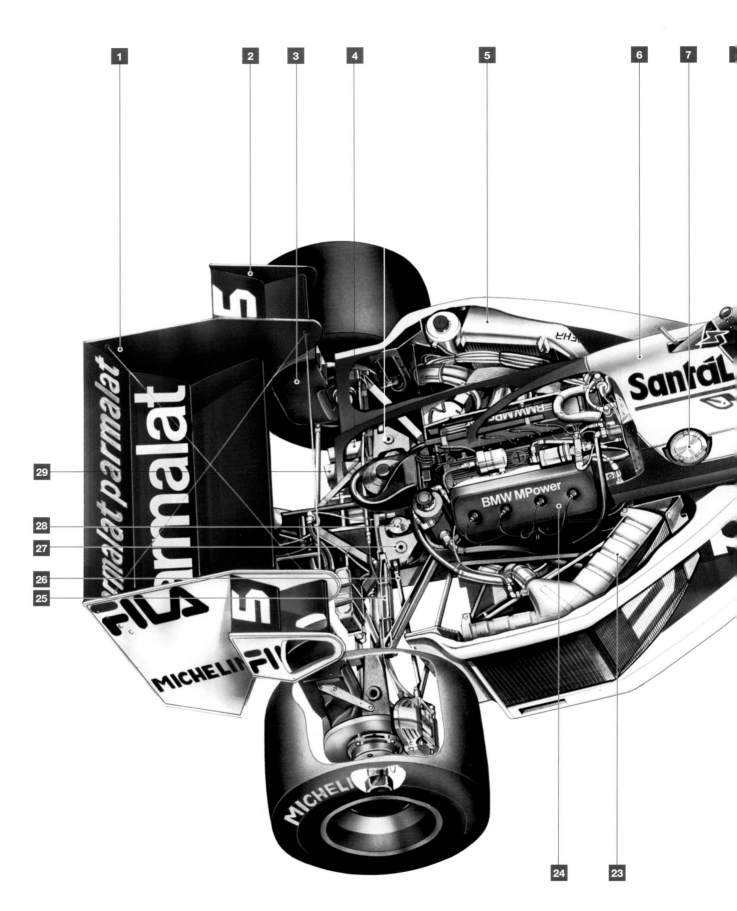

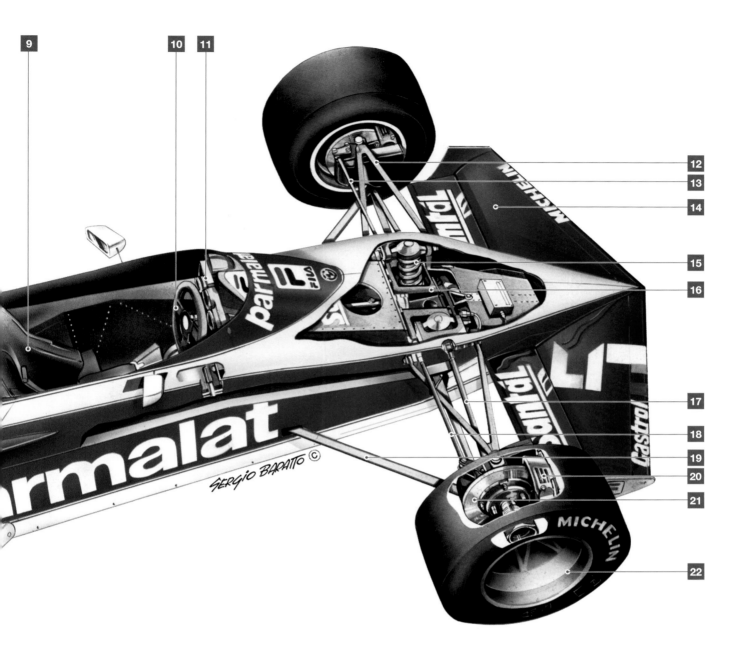

Sergio Baratto's superb illustration shows just how tightly packaged the BT52 was, especially at the rear.
(Sergio Baratto)

1 Rear wing
2 Rear side winglet
3 Rear brake cooling duct
4 Turbo wastegate dump pipe
5 Turbo intercooler
6 Glassfibre engine cover
7 Fuel filler
8 Carbon rollover bar
9 Plastic driver's seat
10 Suede-covered Momo steering wheel
11 Driver's dashboard
12 Front suspension upper wishbone
13 Track-rod
14 Front wing assembly
15 Front coil-over-damper unit
16 Magnesium block casting
17 Front suspension pushrod
18 Track rod
19 Front suspension lower wishbone
20 Front brake caliper
21 Front brake disc
22 13in Momo wheel rim
23 Engine cooling radiator
24 BMW M12/13 engine
25 Rear upper wishbone
26 Rear suspension pushrod
27 Rear suspension rocker
28 Rear coil-over-damper unit
29 Exhaust pipe

bulkhead, which I had had in my mind for some time to try but just never got around to it, so I thought, right, new deal, clean sheet of paper, go for it. The carbon and aluminium monocoque had a thin bulkhead and then I designed a magnesium one-piece casting about 200mm long, all cast, very, very light.

'That was machined and bolted onto studs sticking out of the front of the tub. And that casting had the steering rack, pedal mountings and master cylinder mountings cast into it – all machined. It also had the top rocker and very narrow top wishbone machined into it and it

had the rockers and springs, the anti-roll bar and the bottom front leg of the wishbone cast into it. It was a very elegant, lightweight solution – and that was very new for a racing car.'

At the rear Murray created what he calls the 'race rear end'. Basically everything aft of the rear bulkhead of the monocoque – engine, transmission, rear axle, wing, fuel tank and all associated ancillaries – was attached by four bolts and could be removed as a single unit. This meant that engine changes could be carried out more quickly, and the team would have pre-prepared 'boxes' of replacement rear ends ready to bolt on as required.

'Every night, every team used to work until the early hours of the morning,' Murray says, 'taking the engine and gearbox out, rebuilding the gearbox and final drive, putting in race ratios, checking all the bearings and changing them when needed, and sometimes changing the engine. When I designed the BT49 I did an analysis on why racing cars were failing, and so much of it was guys working at 2am not putting something like a hose clip back on, so I thought how cool it would be if the rear of the car basically just had to be connected to the fuel tank and the throttle and the clutch – and you were off. The BT52 was the world's first car with a back end that is completely self-contained.'

Murray did not go down the full carbon route for the monocoque because he was concerned about its crash behaviour. Crash testing was not officially introduced into Formula 1 until 1985, but a BT50 was subjected to a frontal impact at BMW's test facility (a video of the crash test can be found on YouTube) after Murray had suggested to Ecclestone that he wanted to see what happened in a frontal impact.

As Murray points out, while carbonfibre is exceptionally strong and light, it can also be very brittle. Unlike metal, it cannot be bent back into shape, so considerable care needs to be taken in checking carbonfibre pieces for hairline cracks. Carbonfibre can be repaired, but this obviously depends on the extent of the damage; significant damage to a component as vital as a monocoque would most likely result in it being written off.

The BT52's monocoque design was carried over to the BT53 of 1984 and the BT54 of 1985, together with the front magnesium casing and the race rear end. These elements were only phased out in 1986, when Murray introduced Brabham's first all-carbon monocoque for the radical, if unsuccessful, 'laydown' BT55.

Aerodynamics

With an engine capable of producing well over 800bhp in qualifying mode, the need for a car to be 'slippery' becomes less of a concern. With the BT52, therefore, the principal aim was to create as much downforce as possible, especially at the rear of the car, where it could push the tyres into the ground and harness as much as possible of the explosive engine power.

The narrow point of the BT52's nose meant that the width of the front wing was increased by around 100mm on each side. The wing had just five points of adjustment on the Gurney flap at its rear, from basically flat to almost vertical. The steeper the wing angle, the more

downforce it creates – but it also causes more drag. The more drag a car has, the more power is required to reach its maximum speed. The relationship of downforce to drag has been a constant quandary for all Formula 1 designers since ground effect was outlawed.

The flat underside of the car meant that this area did little, if anything, in terms of downforce, so the rear wing was made as big as possible. No adjustment was permitted for the rear wing – the level of drag and downforce it produced were defined from the outset. However, midway through the season Ferrari found a loophole

ABOVE Brabham introduced these 'winglets' to the BT52B for the European GP to increase rear downforce.
(John Townsend)

RIGHT The 'barn door' rear wing design was possible because of the brute power of the BMW engine. *(Author)*

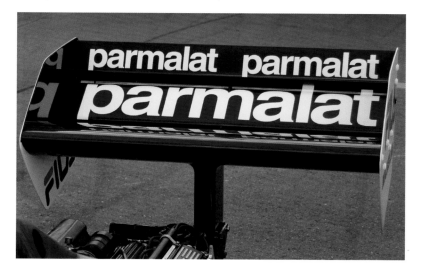

in the regulations and added winglets to the rear wing of its 126C3. This idea was soon incorporated onto the BT52B, with Brabham's version introduced for the European Grand Prix at Brands Hatch.

'We copied the wings on the side – they weren't our idea,' Murray admits. 'We needed all the wing we could get. The rules stated that the rear wing width was only behind the rear wheels, so ahead of the rear wheels you could go out to the body width.'

Unlike modern Formula 1 cars, where CFD studies have resulted in almost every surface having some form of winglet or vane to manage and control the flow of air over the car, the bodywork of the BT52 is flush. The endplates of the front and rear wings are flat, leaving just the wings themselves to produce the downforce.

During the design phase of the BT52, Brabham used the wind-tunnel facilities at Southampton University, while at the same time the team's own tunnel was being constructed at its Chessington factory.

The short timeframe in which the car was designed meant that it spent fewer hours in the wind tunnel than would usually have been the case, but clearly that was no impediment to the car achieving success on track. All the wind-tunnel models were made by Mike Reid, who also cut and fitted the bodywork to the finished full-scale cars.

'On the long sidepods, you still had a proper aerodynamic profile even though skirts had been severely limited by that time,' recalls David North. 'You could still get a lot of downforce. With the flat bottom, however, our thinking at the time was that it was going to be very difficult to generate downforce – you could run the car with a certain amount of rake, but not very much – and we thought there would probably be so much build-up in the boundary layer that the body might even develop upwards force rather than downwards force.

'As there was still scope to have some shaping at the back of the car, we wanted to

get the leading edge as far back as possible and still leave room for a "pseudo" aerofoil section, so that's what we did. We had a model and we used to go down to Southampton University every few weeks. It wasn't desperately efficient, but it looked nice.

'The Southampton tunnel had a rolling road – a big advantage. The air behaves much more realistically than if you have a fixed surface, which creates a boundary layer. Although there are all sorts of things you can do to suck out the boundary layer, if the ground moves with the air you have a much more realistic representation of what the car sees in real life.'

Murray instigated the building of the wind tunnel at Chessington ahead of the 1982 season. However, after receiving quotes that were well above what the team could afford – 'one of them was four years' worth of F1 budget so I didn't even go to Bernie with it' – he set to work to design his own tunnel.

'I read a book on wind-tunnel design,' recalls Murray. 'It didn't seem too complicated so I just designed one according to the book. Nothing clever: the right diffuser angles, the right corner radii, the right turning vanes, the air straighteners – the only thing I had to invent was the rolling road because nobody was doing rolling roads. I think the quote for a rolling road was $4 million and I built one for £160,000.'

The wind tunnel Murray designed is still in action today. After the Brabham factory was sold to Yamaha in the wake of the team's financial collapse, the tunnel was rented out. One of its most high-profile customers was Murray himself when he was working on the McLaren F1 road car. When Yamaha shut down its UK R&D firm – Activa Technology – the factory was sold to Carlin Motorsport, a leading British team that races in GP2, Indy Lights and Renault 3.5. When Carlin hit financial difficulties, the old Brabham factory was taken over by the receivers and subsequently sold off as a series of smaller lots. Meanwhile, the wind tunnel was moved to Carlin's new premises in Farnham,

ABOVE This picture reveals the many components that Murray was able to house within the magnesium bulkhead. *(Author)*

who designed the livery, explains the process.

'The way the colouring of the body was achieved at Brabham was different from most other Formula 1 teams. The initial shape for the body panels was created in the drawing office as a full-size draft, on tracing paper. "Dyeline" prints from these drawings were sent down to the pattern shop, where the pattern makers carved the shape from wood.

'When the correct shape was achieved, we marked out the lines dividing the blue from the white areas. These lines were then cut into the wood with a sharp knife. When the glassfibre tools were taken from the wood pattern, the lines showed up as little upstanding ribs; these ribs were sanded down until they were only a millimetre or so tall.

'At the start of production of a body panel, masking tape was applied on one side of these lines and then dark blue gel-coat [coloured polyester resin] was painted onto the exposed tool surface. The masking tape was then removed and white gel-coat was painted onto the rest of the tool. Before these gel-coat surfaces had hardened, the glass cloth matting was applied using clear resin. Both Gordon Murray and David North reckon that this process saved around 4kg [about 9lb] of paint and was less easily scratched. But taping inside the tool was not so easy!'

The only elements of the livery added after this process were the sponsor decals and the

where it remains to this day. The autoclave that was later built at Brabham, nicknamed 'yellow submarine' on account of its colour, was moved as well and also remains in regular use at Carlin's facility.

Bodywork

The bodywork was made of glassfibre. The team had two versions – lightweight bodywork for use in qualifying and a more heavy-duty version for races. The blue and white colours of Parmalat, the sponsor, were neither painted on nor decals – the colouring was impregnated into the resin. Peter Stevens,

RIGHT The lightweight glassfibre bodywork complete with 'hissing Sid' mascot at the tip of the nose. *(BMW)*

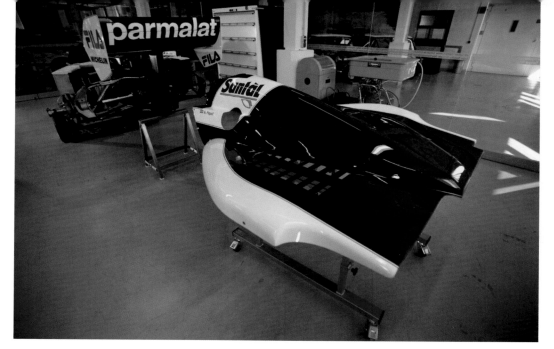

LEFT The cooling vents in the engine cover were added when Brabham discovered overheating issues in pre-season testing. *(BMW)*

dark blue keyline that runs around the car. When the BT52 was launched, the primary colour was white, with dark blue very much the secondary colour. But when he saw the car on TV, Stevens realised that the colour scheme would be more effective if the colours were reversed and informed Ecclestone of his observation. With Bernie's penchant for aesthetics, the revised colours were introduced when the BT52B came on line for the British Grand Prix in July 1983.

The rear-view mirrors were mounted on the bodywork adjacent to the dashboard. These created a problem for Murray, for the narrowness of the car and its lack of sidepods at the point where the mirrors were situated necessitated a crafty solution.

'God knows why, but there was a regulation that said the mirrors had to be within the silhouette of the bodywork,' Murray recalls. 'When you dump the sidepods, of course, the mirrors stick out. When we went for initial scrutineering they said, "You haven't got any bodywork under the mirrors." In fact there was bodywork much wider than the mirrors, but it just happened to be a bit further back.'

Murray's solution was to fit so-called 'silly plates', which were attached to the bodywork at the base of the tub directly beneath each mirror. They looked like they might have been aerodynamic aids, but, as Murray attests, their sole purpose was to get the car to pass scrutineering.

'We shined a light downwards over each mirror and cut out a carbon plate in the shape of the shadow cast by the mirror. Of course, over the years many people walked past and sliced their ankles open on them!'

Cockpit

The cockpit of the BT52 was conventional for a Formula 1 car of its era. Following Niki Lauda's terrible accident at the Nürburgring in 1976, Formula 1 started to analyse the safety of the driver inside the car and by 1983 this had resulted in the creation of the survival cell. This mandated a minimum size for the cockpit aperture, stated that no oil or fuel lines could

BELOW The tiny rearview mirrors on the BT52 required a novel solution to get the car through scrutineering. *(Dirk Daniel Mann/BMW)*

pass through the cockpit, and required the use of a six-point safety harness that the driver could release with one hand.

The seat was made from plastic and individually sculpted to fit the driver. A fire extinguisher was mounted in front of the seat.

On the dashboard there were just three dials – a large rev counter in the middle with a water temperature gauge and a turbo boost gauge on either side.

The suede-covered Momo steering wheel, surprisingly, was not of the quick-release type, which did not become commonplace until the introduction of semi-automatic gearboxes in the early 1990s. Because gear-changing on these

semi-automatic gearboxes was by means of paddle controls mounted on the steering wheel, a quick-release system was convenient in the event of a fault – a common occurrence in their nascent days.

To the driver's right was the gear lever, which was machined from aluminium. The gear-change was arranged in the traditional H-pattern, with five or six speeds used according to the circuit. The short throw required only a flick of the wrist to change gear.

To the driver's left was the turbo boost adjuster. In qualifying mode this would be twisted to 3.0 bar or higher, while for race mode it would typically be around 2.5 bar, although

turning the boost down even lower, as Piquet demonstrated in South Africa, was a viable strategy for conserving the engine as well as for saving fuel.

The pedal box was mounted at the front of the cockpit on the chassis bulkhead. This piece of cast magnesium was one of the few components that remained from the stillborn BT51.

Suspension

The suspension of the BT52, as with all racing cars, was designed to ensure that the car delivered maximum performance at all times. No concessions were made to a driver's comfort.

In 1981 Murray had designed for the BT49 a unique hydraulic suspension system that lowered the car at speed, maximising the downforce from the skirt/ground-effect set-up. When the car slowed it would rise, ensuring that it always passed the mandatory ride-height checks.

As this system became outlawed, the BT52 featured a conventional suspension solution with pushrods. The layout was the same at both ends, but the top wishbones at the rear were aluminium while the lower wishbones at the rear and both top and bottom wishbones at the front were made of steel. Only the

ABOVE The rain light switch was to the driver's left. For 1983 these had been made brighter after Didier Pironi's accident in 1982.
(Dirk Daniel Mann/BMW)

LEFT Fuel pump and ignition switches were to the driver's right and conveniently positioned for hasty use in the event of an engine failure.
(Dirk Daniel Mann/BMW)

LEFT The 'Santal'-liveried 'Gurney' flaps were the only adjustable elements of the front wing – there were just five pre-set positions.
(John Townsend)

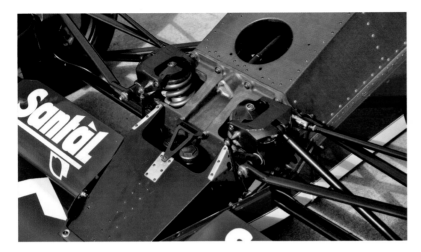

LEFT The Koni coil-over-spring dampers sat within Murray's magnesium casting. *(Dirk Daniel Mann/BMW)*

RIGHT The front brake ducts were attached to the magnesium uprights. *(Dirk Daniel Mann/BMW)*

RIGHT Steel wishbones were used at the top and bottom in the BT52's front suspension. *(BMW)*

front suspension featured an anti-roll bar; the lack of one at the rear was judged helpful for saving weight and for the sake of simplicity. Magnesium uprights and Koni coil-over-damper units completed the set-up.

A coil-over-damper unit comprises a shock absorber with a coil spring encircling it. The shock absorber and spring were assembled as a unit prior to installation. The stiffness of the suspension was changed by using springs of different spring rates.

In modern-day Formula 1, wishbones have evolved to become part of the aerodynamic profile of the cars, but in the 1980s these were simple steel tubes.

Although Murray had introduced pullrod suspension in the 1970s, he opted for pushrods for the BT52. The difference, as the name suggests, is whether the rod pushes up to the rocker or pulls down from the rocker. The pullrod set-up has a strut from the outer end of each upper wishbone that runs diagonally to the lower edge of the chassis and 'pulls' a rocker to operate the spring/damper unit. A pushrod is the opposite – the strut runs from the lower wishbone to the upper edge of the chassis.

As with the uprights, the rockers were made of cast magnesium. At the front these were part of the single-piece magnesium casting bolted to the front bulkhead. The system did not leave a great deal of flexibility for adjustment, but this was intentional, as Murray explains.

'There was stuff you could change – the spring and damper ratings. But the incidence of the car suddenly wasn't that important any more. With ground effect, a millimetre made a difference so you had to get the ride height just right. But once you didn't have sidepods and skirts, you didn't need all this fine adjustment. I

LEFT The pushrod suspension has a rocker connected to the spring/damper unit mounted in the magnesium casting. *(Author)*

don't think we ever had a race where the driver said the car didn't handle.'

David North has further observations: 'The whole car was pretty unadjustable, which was a Gordon thing that I sort-of shared with him. The car was designed to avoid any more complication than necessary.

'The less there is, the less there is to go wrong. Normally with anti-roll bars – and certainly on cars of that era – you end up with the front bar significantly stiffer than the rear bar, and you can get similar balance of roll stiffness if you just take away the rear bar altogether and subtract that amount of stiffness from the front bar. You can do everything you need to do with just the front bar. So that's what we did.

'We also used to try to get the spring rate right. We used to think more about suspension frequencies than they do now. Both ends of a car have an undamped bounce frequency and we used to try to get the front and rear frequencies in the same ballpark. In that you had more weight at the back, you'd have stiffer springs at the back – if you pushed down on the car without any dampers the front and rear would have the same frequency in terms of cycles per second.'

An anti-roll bar is intended to force each side of the car to drop, or rise, to similar heights, so as to reduce the sideways tilting (roll) of the car through corners or over bumps. This maximises the amount of tyre that is in contact with the road at any given time to ensure that maximum grip is achieved.

Given that there was little scope to adjust the anti-roll bar to refine the handling, the team had the option to use 'packers' to alter the handling balance. These packers would be placed inside the springs to adjust the rate at which the

LEFT The front anti-roll bar (not pictured) is also mounted in the magnesium casting at the front end. *(Author)*

LEFT Spring rates could be changed to fine tune the handling of the BT52. *(Author)*

RIGHT The steering arm (left) is made from steel.
(Author)

ABOVE The suspension would be crack-tested after each session and replaced after a specified distance had been covered. *(Author)*

ABOVE RIGHT The rocker (left) had to be removed to give access to the spring/damper unit. *(Author)*

BELOW The splined hole close to the track towards the bottom of the gearbox casing is where the starter was inserted to fire the car into life. *(Author)*

springs bounced. This system is still employed to great effect in NASCAR stock car racing in the US to this day.

'We typically used Koni's nylon discs in conjunction with their yellow foam bump stops,' North recalls. 'Each disc was a defined thickness, whereas the conical bump stops had a bit of squidge. Cars these days tend to be very stiff at the front. They have these huge front wings and it's all about trying to keep the

front wing as close to the ground as possible. In those days the front-to-rear aero was governed by ride height.'

The pushrods were of a set length, so any adjustment of ride height came from the pre-load that was put into the springs. Spring pre-loading refers to the amount of compression applied to the spring before the mass of the car is added. A compressed spring is shorter than a non-compressed one.

Changing the front springs was very simple. First the rockers had to be removed and set aside. There was a 5mm aluminium pin at the bottom of each spring/damper unit to provide location in the magnesium casting and once this pin was out the spring/damper unit could just be lifted out and a new unit dropped back in.

Another unusual feature of the BT52's rear suspension was the absence of adjustment for toe-in. This meant that a cylindrical joint could be used instead of a spherical joint, saving significant weight. Toe-in refers to the angle of the wheels relative to the centre line of the chassis: if a wheel runs perfectly parallel to the centre line there is no toe-in; if it is angled towards the centre line it has toe-in; and if it is angled away from the centre line it has toe-out. Toe angles can be used to affect tyre wear, stability and handling.

The wishbones were checked after every session to ensure that no cracks had developed, while the entire suspension set-up was stripped down and rebuilt ahead of each event. All suspension parts were attributed with a specific life span measured in distance and a component would be replaced once the given distance was approaching. Dampers needed to be regularly checked to ensure that bump and rebound rates correlated.

Brakes

Brabham introduced carbonfibre brakes – of Dunlop manufacture – to Formula 1 on the BT45, the Alfa Romeo-powered car it raced during the 1976 season, and by 1983 the use of carbonfibre brakes had become commonplace. Most teams used brakes from AP, but Brabham's supplier was now Girling.

The advantage of carbonfibre brakes – with both discs and calipers made from the composite material – is that they are able to operate at higher temperatures for longer than steel or cast-iron discs and calipers. This meant that they gave the driver more consistent feel, were less susceptible to fade, and delivered more consistent performance. They were also fitted with smaller calipers than had been used with brakes of steel or cast iron.

The downside is that carbonfibre brakes also take longer to warm up, so drivers need to be mindful of this and keep generating heat into the brakes where possible. Also the higher operating temperatures of the carbonfibre brakes mean they require more cooling.

To keep the brakes from overheating, Brabham did a great deal of work with cooling. Brake ducts were devised to channel cool air into the braking system at front and rear. At the front these were mounted outboard of the magnesium upright and in between the upper and lower suspension wishbones. At the rear, with the area in front of the wheel covered by the short sidepods, the cooling ducts were funnelled up through this bodywork to create 'ears'.

Extreme care needs to be taken when

BELOW Brabham had used carbon brakes since 1976. By 1983 the team was using Girling discs and pads. *(John Townsend)*

BOTTOM The degree of cooling required varied from track to track. Where less was needed, the duct was covered up – as here – to reduce the cooling effect and drag. *(BMW)*

handling carbonfibre brakes: they can reach temperatures of 1,000°C during use and although they cool quickly from this peak they can still be around 400°C when a car stops in the pits.

To save weight in qualifying, Brabham used to fit smaller, lighter brakes. More durable versions were put on for the race, and larger discs and calipers were available for circuits that made greater braking demands. Between qualifying and the race, discs, pads and calipers were replaced, and a complete new set of brake components was fitted between every grand prix.

Braking in a Formula 1 car is strongly biased towards the front because of the weight transfer to the front produced under the extreme loading that braking produces. The driver was able to adjust the brake bias from inside the cockpit.

Hydraulic brake fluid was contained in a pair of master cylinders located in the magnesium bulkhead casting in the nose of the car, just ahead of the dampers. A small radiator was positioned directly ahead of the master cylinders in order to provide cooling for the brake fluid.

When the driver pushes the brake pedal, brake fluid is pushed into the caliper's cylinders and the carbon brake disc is squeezed between the carbon brake blocks. The resulting friction causes the disc and wheel to slow down. It is this friction that causes the heat to build up. The ability to cope with this heat is why carbon brakes are more efficient.

Transmission

The transmission of a racing car is fundamentally the same as that of a road car in that it comprises a gearbox, clutch, differential and drive shafts. However, for a car such as the BT52, these components have to be designed to deal with much higher stresses due to the extreme amount of torque generated by the turbo engine.

In the BT52, the gearbox was a five- or six-speed manual, with a traditional H-pattern shift. The number of gears depended on the requirements of the circuit.

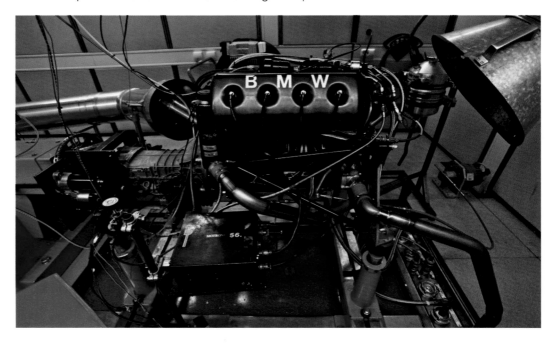

The casing of the gearbox was designed by Brabham and machined in magnesium. The internals came from Hewland's FT200 range, while the differential was a bespoke design built in a collaboration between Brabham and Pete Weismann, the Californian-based transmission specialist. The Brabham-made gearbox casing also included the bellhousing and contained the hydraulically controlled carbonfibre clutch. The bellhousing also doubled as the engine oil tank.

The gearbox was mounted longitudinally onto the rear of the engine, where it also provided mounting points for the rear suspension wishbones and the rear wing supports. As was the case with the whole of the BT52's 'race rear end', the entire transmission was self-contained within the rear structure, including lubrication and cooling systems.

The FT200 was one of Hewland's best-selling gearboxes, with over 2,000 units sold since its introduction in 1966. It was used in a variety of single-seaters, but was chosen by Brabham for the BT52 because of its compact size and light weight.

Because of the amount of power that went through the transmission, different gearboxes were used for qualifying and the race. Murray's 'race rear end' concept meant that gearboxes could be prepared in advance, so that when the 'qualifying rear end' was removed and the 'race rear end' bolted on, the gearbox was ready to go.

The gear ratios would often be changed late in the proceedings, with the wind conditions of the day an important factor in determining the ratios.

To ensure that gearboxes were as reliable as possible, as soon as a car's rear end was removed, the gearbox was taken out, stripped down and rebuilt. After qualifying in particular, many of the internals needed to be replaced. After a gearbox was rebuilt, it was mounted into the rear end that would be used either in qualifying or for the next race.

Because of the abundant power going through the transmission, the differential needed to be able to handle extreme loads – and the design of differential used in the BT52 was huge by modern standards. Designed in

ABOVE The BMW Motorsport crew winch the M12/13 into the air during the rebuild process. *(BMW)*

LEFT The clutch – large by today's F1 standards – is clearly visible in this view of the BMW engine. *(BMW)*

conjunction with Weismann, it uses cam-and-pawl technology.

The cam-and-pawl concept was one of the earliest forms of limited slip differentials, which had come to prominence during the 1970s. The cam-and-pawl system creates a locking differential, with the diff locking with applied torque, driving both wheels as a spool. This occurs as the pawls are forced into the notches in the inner cam track and outer cam track, which causes the differential to lock.

The advantage of the cam-and-pawl system is that its lock-up is predictable, occurring whenever power is applied. This is especially useful when a car has a lot of power, as with the BT52, and the driver tends to use a 'point-and-squirt' technique, rather than trying to carry all possible speed through the corner.

The differential was fully serviced after each race, with the pawls often needing to be changed due to the extreme loads put through them. The same applied to the drive shafts, which were made of conventional steel on the BT52, and needed examination and replacement after every race.

BELOW The extreme heat from the exhaust means the left-rear suspension has heat shield material wrapped around it. *(Author)*

In 1983 Brabham had a deal with Castrol for the development and supply of lubricants. The team utilised B373, a mineral-based gearbox and differential oil that is renowned for its high performance and load-carrying ability, and remains available today.

'We were very fortunate that season,' recalls Roly Vincini, who was in charge of transmissions. 'I think we had a loss of crown wheel and pinion on Piquet's car at Spa, but otherwise I don't think we lost races because of a gearbox problem. But you had to change the internals and maintain a gearbox after the right time period – it wouldn't last much longer than a weekend.'

Engine

While the distinctive appearance of the Brabham BT52 is what stays in people's minds, BMW's four-cylinder turbocharged engine was its defining component. It was the expectation of the horsepower the 1.5-litre four-cylinder engine was going to produce that convinced Murray to shift so much of the car's componentry to the back, creating the unique

and beautiful 'paper dart' look. And it was the sheer grunt of the M12/13 engine that carried Piquet to two wins in the last three races of 1983, and brought home that year's drivers' World Championship.

The origins of the M12/13 engine lie in a design from Baron Alex von Falkenhausen, who was asked by BMW to design a small-capacity engine that would be suitable for the new range of cars the Munich-based company was producing. He initially presented a straight-four, single-overhead-camshaft, 1.3-litre motor, but this was considered to be too small, so the capacity was increased to 1.5 litres, with the potential to enlarge it to 2 litres. This engine became known as the M10 and was manufactured in huge numbers, powering over 3.5 million BMW road cars in various guises from launch in 1962 until it was phased out in 1988.

In the late 1960s, when Formula 2 regulations were changed to allow 1.6-litre engines, BMW built a four-valve version of the M10 engine and started racing it. This engine was developed by Paul Rosche into the M12 for 1969, when BMW also started to develop its own chassis. This project was short-lived and BMW went back to just supplying engines.

The various iterations of the M12 engine enjoyed an amazing level of success in the 1970s, taking the European Formula 2 Championship title six times – in 1973, 1974, 1975, 1978, 1979 and then again in 1982 – and by the time of the last title the engine had evolved into the M12/7.

In 1973 BMW introduced the first road car in Europe with a turbocharged engine. This was the 2002 Turbo and the engine was a version of the M12. Rosche again developed a version of this for the *Deutsche Rennsport Meisterschaft* (DRM), Germany's domestic touring car championship that was a forerunner of today's *Deutsche Tourenwagen Masters* (DTM). The DRM was run to Group 5 regulations, which stipulated that turbocharged engines were limited to a size of 1.4 litres. It was the success, and power, that BMW derived from these engines that gave rise to thoughts of Formula 1.

'We found out that we could get very good power,' says Rosche. 'With this engine we could reach 550bhp, so we thought it was possible to make out of this engine a Formula 1 engine.

BELOW BMW's M12/13 engine has its origins in a road car engine from the 1960s! *(Dirk Daniel Mann/BMW)*

a capacity of 1,499cc. The engine block was made of iron, while the head, now fitted with double overhead camshafts, was of aluminium. There were four valves per cylinder – two inlet, two outlet. The crankshaft was made of steel, while the Mahle pistons were forged alloy with their heads cooled from underneath by an oil spray. The H-shaped connecting rods were made of titanium to enable them to withstand the extreme loads that were created.

This was the first Formula 1 engine to feature electronic management and Bosch provided the system. The fuel-metering unit was based on a Kugelfischer design that was adapted by Bosch to work with the ECU. The system employed a Bosch electric high-pressure pump for getting the engine started and a Lucas mechanical pump, for normal running, mounted on the inlet camshaft and driven directly by the camshaft gear.

The M12/13 engine was installed in the BT52 by means of a steel frame and an aluminium front plate that was attached to the monocoque by four bolts. Mounted behind the engine was the single KKK (Kühnle, Kopp & Kausch) turbo, a cast-iron unit originally from a turbo-diesel truck, with its associated wastegate. The Behr intercooler was located to the left of the engine. To the right of the engine was a single integral radiator, also by Behr, to cool both oil and water. Underneath the engine was a carbonfibre undertray.

We knew the power output from the Cosworth engine was around 450bhp and this was the point we thought to do something in Formula 1. It was a good result from the 1.4 litre.'

Through the development of the M12, the bore – the diameter of the cylinder – always remained the same at 89.2mm. It was the stroke – the distance the piston travels – that defined the displacement.

Once the BMW board had approved the Formula 1 project (see Chapter Two), Rosche and his team set about developing the engine.

With a stroke of 60mm, the M12/13 had

In total the engine and its ancillaries weighed around 170kg (375lb).

The engine underwent three main areas of development – electronics, turbo and fuel.

Throughout the competitive life of the engine, one of the biggest challenges was getting the electronics correct. These were the early days of electronic management systems and the Bosch version used on the M12/13 employed 'e-prom' chip technology. The ECU (Electronic Control Unit) was used to control a series of processes in the engine, including the mixture of air and fuel in the combustion chamber and the timing of the ignition. All of this information was 'hard-coded' onto the e-prom chip. Once the information was programmed in, the chip was burned – and thereafter there was no opportunity for adjustment. If a small miscalculation had been made, the result could be disastrous – and this is what happened at Detroit in 1982 when Piquet failed to qualify in the BT50.

'We had a big problem with our electronics,' Rosche admits of that Detroit weekend. 'On Friday we were very bad and we had no laps. On Saturday the engine was running but it was raining and we didn't qualify. It was a big disaster. One week later we had Montréal. On Friday and Saturday we had a constant misfire. So before the race we changed everything on the car, especially the loom and the electronics, and suddenly the engine was running and we won our first race. It was a wonder, believe me. We took everything back to Munich and put the engine on the dyno – and it didn't work. I never really found out what the problem was.'

When the M12/13 engine finally hit the track in 1982, the drivers initially struggled with the turbo lag – the time that elapses between pressing the accelerator pedal and the turbocharger providing increased intake pressure and hence increased power. This lag occurs because a turbocharger relies on the build-up of exhaust-gas pressure to drive its turbine. In the early days of turbocharging, lag

ABOVE **The engines were hand-built by BMW Motorsport in Munich.** (BMW)

was a common complaint from drivers who were used to the instantaneous power delivery of normally aspirated engines.

For those manufacturers using a V6 turbo, namely Ferrari and Renault (and Honda when it joined in mid-1983), the solution was a twin-turbo set-up, with one smaller turbo and one larger one; the small one built up pressure quickly to provide the initial power while the larger one spooled up.

Rosche tried this solution on the M12/13, but it did not deliver the results as effectively on the four-cylinder engine as it did on V6s. Instead, his

RIGHT **The straight-four, cast-iron block of the M12/13.** (BMW)

LEFT The aluminium cylinder head for the M12/13 engine. *(BMW)*

solution was to introduce an extra butterfly valve – a type of valve that oscillates inside a pipe to regulate flow – to the turbocharging system.

'We had four butterflies in the normal position before the valves,' Rosche explains, 'and we added one more larger butterfly before the turbocharger. We had a link between the single butterfly and the four butterflies, and closing the large one before the smaller ones helped us a lot with the throttle response.'

Rosche tried to persuade BMW to build a V6 turbo in 1983, but funding was not forthcoming.

LEFT The four overhead valves for each cylinder are in situ in the head. *(BMW)*

BELOW LEFT The cam cover is replaced before the rebuild process progresses. *(BMW)*

BELOW Castrol developed all the lubricants for the BMW turbo F1 engines. *(BMW)*

Knowing that he simply had to make the best of what he was given, he set about maximising the M12/13 engine's key advantage – its massive KKK turbocharger.

Once Brabham had mastered its mid-race refuelling, the team noticed that, if the car had been stopped for too long, there was a high chance of a turbo failure in the laps after the stop. This was because the turbo bearings overheated while the car was stationary. Brabham's solution was to take a bleed off the line from the air jacks so that cool air was blown onto the bearings – to reduce the risk of their subsequent seizure – while the car was jacked up.

BMW had two engine modes in 1983 – one for qualifying, the other for the race. In qualifying everything was turned up to the maximum setting, which in 1983 meant boost – the pressure of the air forced into the inlet manifold – of around 3.5 bar or just over 50 pounds per square inch. At higher pressure, the air becomes more combustible, which makes the detonations in the cylinders more explosive, which in turn creates greater force at the crankshaft.

Coupled with this, for qualifying the team would remove the wastegate, shovel dry ice into the intercooler, and advance the ignition by a degree or two. The most extreme version of this procedure was nicknamed 'Hitler mode' by one of the BMW crew, and if something went wrong when in 'Hitler mode' the consequences would be spectacular.

'We heard the explosion,' Murray says, 'when the car was at the right-hander just behind the pits at Zolder. A conrod pushed the crankshaft and literally split the block in half – a cast-iron BMW block that had been aged for a year outside to strengthen it. The block was split all the way around and the crank was pushed into the road, making a big hole that caused the car to break in half!

'I said to Paul, who is a genius, "In case you haven't noticed, we've got a race in a couple of weeks and we just split a block in half. We like 'Hitler mode' and we don't want to dump it, so what are you going to do?"

'Paul got the mould for the block and had somebody put some ribs in the side of it. And so BMW was able to cast some special blocks with ribs – and we never had the problem again.'

In its most extreme state, the engine could deliver more than 1,000bhp. But such engines did not last long – two qualifying runs if the driver was lucky. In the race the boost was reduced to around 2.5 bar, which produced around 750bhp. The driver could adjust boost pressure during a race, and Piquet often did so to preserve the engine.

After every race, all engines used in qualifying and the race were sent back to Germany to be stripped down and rebuilt. Special attention was always paid to the pistons and rods, which would always be changed as a matter of course. Valves and valve springs would be checked and probably replaced, as would all other moving parts.

As with the transmission, Castrol developed a special oil to cope with the demands of the

ABOVE BMW M power went up to over 1,400bhp on later versions of the M12/13 engine. (BMW)

BELOW The finishing touch as the engine rebuild is completed. (BMW)

high-revving – 11,500rpm – engine. This was called B353, a formulation of castor oil that was designed to prevent oxidants building up in the combustion chambers.

That was not the only formulation that would play a key role in the success of the BT52. There was also a fascinating fuel development. Formula 1 regulations stipulated that fuel could not exceed 102RON, where RON stands for Research Octane Number and the number refers to the amount of pressure the fuel can withstand before self-igniting – the higher the number, the greater the pressure it can accept.

Midway through the 1983 season a contact of Rosche's who worked for Wintershall, a subsidiary of chemical giant BASF, came across a batch of synthetic fuel that the company had developed for Second World War fighter aircraft. As Germany during wartime had lacked sufficient lead to create the usual blend of fuel needed for high-performance engines, a lead substitute – Toluene – had been manufactured, and this is what Rosche's contact found.

Toluene was mixed with iso-octane and n-heptane to create a fuel that was below the 102RON prescribed by the rules, but provided much better detonation than the standard race fuel the team had been using previously. The better detonation allowed the team to run higher boost and thus race with more horsepower. This helped Brabham to win the last three races of 1983 and Piquet to take the title.

A rival fuel supplier claimed to have taken a sample of the fuel used at Kyalami, the last race of the 1983 season, and to have discovered that its RON was far higher than 102. But no protest was ever made and the Brabham cars passed the official post-race checks.

There is no doubt that the fuel was a highly toxic blend and the Brabham mechanics who worked most closely with it often suffered nosebleeds. Inspired by what BMW and BASF did in 1983, race fuels in Formula 1 became ever more exotic in subsequent years until

ABOVE The radiators were mounted either side of the engine in the very short sidepods. *(John Townsend)*

BELOW The water radiator – mounted in the right-hand side sidepod – is the bigger of the two. *(Dirk Daniel Mann/BMW)*

BUILDING THE AWESOME BMW ENGINE

During the 1982 season, in the week separating the German Grand Prix and the race in Austria, the Brabham team was invited to pay a visit to BMW Motorsport in Bavaria.

The vast majority of the race team made the trip to see how the M12/13 turbo engines were produced, and to get to know their counterparts in Munich.

The Brabham boys were treated to some fine Bavarian hospitality. After touring BMW's motorsport museum – which is where BT52 chassis No.1 now resides – they were invited into the factory and Paul Rosche's office, where the key decisions on the development of the engine were made.

It was here they discovered that when the first BMW engine was sent to Brabham's Chessington factory, ostensibly so the

ABOVE The M12/13 on the dynamometer in Munich.

(John Townsend)

LEFT The Brabham team was invited to see the engine being manufactured.

(John Townsend)

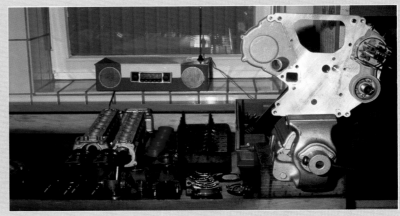

ABOVE The team was given a complete behind -the-scenes tour. *(John Townsend)*

ABOVE At some point Kraftwerk and The Scorpions must have blared out of that radio! *(John Townsend)*

BELOW the Brabham team was impressed by the attention to detail of the BMW technicians. *(John Townsend)*

BELOW BMW introduced its full team to their Brabham counterparts. *(John Townsend)*

BOTTOM Many of the BMW team members who worked on the engine in 1982 were part of the 2013 rebuild project. *(John Townsend)*

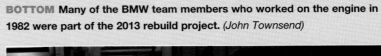

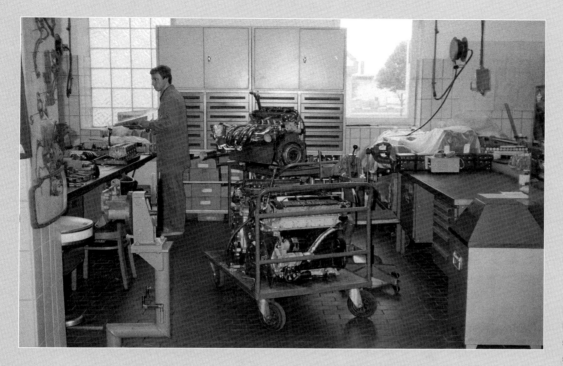

LEFT The next batch of M12/13 engines is prepared for delivery. *(John Townsend)*

BELOW LEFT Brabham was BMW's sole team in 1982, but supply was expanded to ATS for 1983. *(John Townsend)*

BELOW Note the beer bottles and glasses on the desk in the background of this photograph – very Bavarian! *(John Townsend)*

team could understand the dimensions and installation requirements of the motor, BMW had assumed that the Brabham mechanics would open the engine up to have a peek inside.

With this in mind, they took out the pistons and replaced them with bottles of beer. It was only when the engine was subsequently returned with the beer undrunk they realised that their English partners weren't quite as curious as they expected!

Still, this situation was soon remedied in Munich, as John Townsend, Brabham's main photographer at the time, and the man responsible for most of the fantastic images in this book, recalls.

"They took us to a traditional bierkeller. As is the case in Germany, everyone was there from the cleaner to the managing director and you had no idea who you could be sitting next to. It was a great way to meet everybody."

eventually these brews were outlawed and standard pump fuel became mandatory.

Earlier in this section Murray mentioned the matter of the cast-iron engine block becoming stronger with age. Rosche adds more on this point.

'It was very important for the performance of the engine that we had completely round bores,' says Rosche. 'When a block was new the bores were slightly elliptical, but with an engine that had done maybe 100,000km the bore was much better – but the problem then was to reduce the oil consumption of the engine.

'Later, with new blocks, we used to run them three or four times through an oven, and that would take out of them all of the stressed material.'

And, to conclude, there have long been unsubstantiated rumours that BMW mechanics used to urinate on the blocks to help with the aging process...

Wheels and tyres

Once the flat-bottom regulations for 1983 had been rubber-stamped and it became clear that turbo power rather than ground effect was going to rule the roost, Murray took the decision that a switch to Michelin radial tyres was required.

Although Brabham had won the 1981 World Championship on Goodyear tyres, it was felt that Michelin's radial-ply construction was better suited than Goodyear's cross-ply rubber to handling the power of BMW's turbo engine.

Michelin introduced radials to Formula 1 in 1977 with Renault at the same time as the French car giant brought turbocharging to the fore. The difference in the two types of construction is explained in the names. On a radial tyre the plies that form the carcass are radially oriented, which means that they run across the tyre from side to side, at 90 degrees to the direction of travel. In a cross-ply tyre the carcass plies intersect and form an approximate 45-degree angle to the direction of travel.

Most of the advantage of a radial tyre over a cross-ply comes from its strong but flexible sidewall. Having already run radial tyres at Le Mans, Michelin was aware that its tyres had in-built superiority in terms of tread rigidity. In racing terms this made for better braking and,

especially, better traction, which with over 700bhp going through the rear wheels was going to make a key difference.

When the BT52 completed its first test, it was on Avon rubber as the Michelin deal had yet to be completed, but by the time the cars arrived in Brazil for the first official test and the opening race of the season, they were equipped with Michelin radials.

With rear traction paramount, there was a huge difference in tyre size between the front and rear. Mounted on lightweight 13in Momo wheels, the front tyres were 23/62 x 13X while the rears were a chunky 40/66 x 13X.

Pierre Dupasquier looked after Michelin's Formula 1 programme at the time and he recalls the challenge of building tyres for the super-powerful racers.

'We have two major ways to work on tyres,' he states. 'The first is the size, width and diameter, because this makes what we put on the ground. More important is the diameter, because you use 100 per cent of what you increase. But with width you don't benefit 100 per cent, because the car is moving, because of camber changes, because of the displacement of the tread compared to the rim, and so on.

'The other thing is compound. But compound is a trap unless you make a major discovery. Like for everyday tyres: if you increase longevity in the dry you lose in the wet; if you increase in the wet, you lose in the dry. So the problem is that unless you make such an invention that you win everywhere, you are trapped in having a harder compound that is stronger but has less grip and slides more, or a softer compound where you grip more but the wear is higher.

'In Formula 1 we thought we had freedom on the rules, but not really. We could not come up with a tyre like an earthmover! And those guys went from 400/500bhp to 700bhp and more, which was a major change for us. In addition we had to cope with the loss of downforce – the more downforce we have the happier we are. With more downforce the car has more grip and doesn't slip, doesn't slide. With the extra torque of the turbo engine we did everything we could. We reinforced the construction of the tyres for the load. We had a lot of different compounds to balance traction and longevity.'

Brabham's decision to make a mid-race pit-stop and change tyres took some of the pressure off the need for tyre longevity. While not all of the teams followed suit in refuelling in 1983, all did go along with the notion of stopping for fresh tyres. As part of his calculations that led to the decision to refuel, Murray understood that his plan could only work if the tyres that were fitted were already up to race temperature. Thus the Brabham team set about designing Formula 1's first tyre warmers.

'We had this oven that looked like Dr Who's Tardis,' says Murray. 'It was a blue thing with a gas fire in the bottom, vents at the top, and holes opposite each tyre – two rears and two fronts – where we could probe the tyre to check temperature. More than once we cooked the compound before we got the tyres out!

'But without this our plan wouldn't have worked. We knew the ideal temperatures from the tyre manufacturer – when the tyre started working, when it was cooked, when it stopped working because it was too hot. So we knew the limits. And we knew what temperatures the tyres were running because we used to check them the moment a driver stopped in the pits – our drivers came in really quickly on purpose.'

On each of the cars Michelin supplied – Renault, Alfa Romeo, McLaren, Ligier and Osella also used its tyres – the company was intrigued to understand what was working and why. Yet despite having to supply so many teams, Michelin was able to offer an almost bespoke service to each of them.

'We were fortunate at that time to have complete freedom with tyres and with that you can create a product that's a marvel for an engineer,' Dupasquier remembers. 'There were no rules about the number of tyres or anything like that. So we could select per team the right tyre for the car – only Michelin has ever done this in the whole of Formula 1 history. Nobody was as curious as we were, and I was always trying to understand what was going on.

'We had lots of different tyres in our truck – and sometimes some difficulties with the teams! We always had an extra set of a different kind in case a team was in trouble. It was an internal rule at Michelin. We knew we were developing as fast as we could for each team at the circuit, and we had an extra opportunity to not disadvantage somebody if they made a mistake – and everybody knew that.'

Nowadays when BMW's own BT52 (see Chapter Seven) takes part in demonstration runs, it is equipped with Avon tyres. Avon has long supported the historic racing scene and supplies a number of tyres suitable for mid-1980s turbo-era cars. Michelin is also able to supply historic tyres, but as these are built to order they are expensive.

Refuelling

The idea of pitting for extra fuel had been commonplace in the early days of the Formula 1 World Championship, but by the late 1950s the practice had been phased out, the teams having calculated that it would be faster to run the race on a single tank of fuel rather than lose time for a pit-stop.

For the next 25 years pit-stops were a rare sight in Formula 1, usually only taking place when a driver had suffered a puncture or a

BELOW The famous 'beer barrel' refuelling rig that Brabham built for 1982.
(John Townsend)

mechanical problem, or if there was a change in track conditions from dry to wet or *vice versa*. When these stops did take place, they usually meant the driver had lost the race and they were fraught, slightly shambolic affairs – watch the footage of James Hunt's stop during the 1976 Japanese Grand Prix for proof of this.

But while scheduled pit-stops fell out of fashion in Formula 1, they remained a staple part of sports-car and Indycar racing. After his Eureka moment about refuelling, Murray paid a visit to the Indy 500 and his mind was made up.

Once the decision had been made, the team needed a refuelling rig. As was usually the case with the Brabham team of that era, they decided to develop their own refuelling rig rather than buy an off-the-peg version. Their solution sounds like a Heath Robinson contraption but in fact it was highly effective.

Brabham's refuelling rig utilised two aluminium beer barrels, one of which – according to legend – was found in a hedge by team personnel on their way to the pub. These barrels were pressurised to 80psi using nitrogen. One carried the fuel while the other served as an accumulator for the air forced out of the BT52's tank as the pressurised fuel was forced in. The car's 42-gallon tank could be filled in just five seconds!

A compressed air cylinder fed each of the barrels via a regulator. A massive Aeroquip pipe linked the two barrels, running between the top of the air barrel and the top of the fuel barrel. A huge flexible pipe with a nozzle fitting on the end – kit adapted from an aircraft fuelling rig – was fixed to the bottom of the fuel barrel, and an adjacent red lever could be operated to stop the flow of fuel in the event of something going wrong.

On each side of the car were two Avery Hardoll hose clippings. One side was used to put the fuel in, while the other side served to take the air out – which side was which depended on the layout of the pit and pitlane.

This rig itself consisted of two packhorses on wheels. One carried the air bottle and air cylinder, while the other was for the fuel line and fuel barrel. At races the two units were clipped together and connected via the big Aeroquip pipe.

Once they had the equipment, the team just needed to learn how to use it. Initial testing took place at Donington, but practice runs there with a BT50 did not always run smoothly,

as Rupert Manwaring, the man who held the fuel nozzle, recalls.

'The sequence of actions was this. You pushed on the connector and turned it through 90 degrees to lock it. Simultaneously Bill Wotherspoon, who was on the other side of the car, connected a venting pipe with a catch tank and a vent to take away the air. So if I went on first and turned before he did the same thing, the thing would pressurise the tank and blow the chassis up.

'Obviously we were trying to cut this down to the last second and on one occasion at Paul Ricard we overfilled the fuel tank. The fuel blocked the air vent effectively and that caused the tank to blow up, which then blew the bottom out of the chassis.'

The team intended to make its first mid-race fuel stop at the 1982 British Grand Prix, but it took until Austria, three races later, for a BT50 to make it far enough into a race for the pit-stop to be attempted.

While the Paul Ricard incident caused significant damage to the car, the team was never really in any danger. This was not the case when they attempted a practice stop in testing at Rio ahead of the 1983 Brazilian race.

'We were testing and still getting used to the system,' Manwaring recalls. 'We were trying a new sight tube. Basically when I saw the fuel coming to an end and turning mainly to froth, I would disconnect the fuel side and Bill would disconnect the air-vent side.

'We were experimenting with the sight tubes and on this particular occasion we were in the pits in Rio. The car hadn't run so it was cold, but the ambient temperature was probably 40°C and we were just standing around in shorts and flip-flops. We thought we'd do a test run, and as I was walking towards the car – the system was fully pressurised – I could see the sight tube growing in length.

'Whatever material we had decided to use wasn't strong enough and just as I got to the car the sight tube burst! It was just like a cartoon, with this flailing snake going around the garage squirting fuel. Luckily I think there was only about ten gallons in it as it was only a test run. But Pete McKenzie, Bill, me and a few others found ourselves standing there dripping in fuel in scorching heat. Luckily Pete wasn't smoking,

which was unusual, and we all ran outside and the fuel evaporated, so we got away with it.'

During the initial practices, Murray would film the pit-stop routines and then analyse where time was being lost and try to devise ways to make the procedure more efficient. Initially this resulted in better wheel guns and wheel nuts so that the wheels could be removed and reattached faster. Later this brought about the introduction of air jacks, which did away with the need for manual jacking.

The air jacks – one at the front of the car and two at the rear – popped down from within the floor of the car and lifted it so that the wheels could be changed. The system was operated by the insertion of a large syringe-like probe into an aperture in the rear bodywork. This pressurised the system, forcing the jacks down, while the air pumped in was also used to cool the turbo (see page 87).

The fuel tank itself, apart from being smaller than usual at 42 gallons, was a standard ATL (Aero Tech Laboratories) product with baffles in it. Baffles are dividers that sit within the lower part of the tank and stop the fuel from sloshing around. The use of a tank with baffles was particularly important on the BT52 as it gave the team a degree of flexibility in the timing of a pit-stop as the car was still able to run when fuel level was getting low.

The refuelling rig needed to be carefully dismantled and stored, but did not require any specific maintenance over and above a good level of housekeeping to ensure that everything was clean and functioning properly.

The combination of a well-drilled crew and good equipment meant that the Brabham team led the way in pit-stop times. The process took around 15 seconds at the introduction of refuelling but by the end of the 1983 season the team was able to accomplish a stop in under ten seconds. But this advantage was short-lived as refuelling was outlawed for 1984.

Tyre changing, however, remained a key part of Formula 1 and Brabham kept up its disciplined approach. In 1987, many of the team who worked on the BT52 were part of the crew who appeared on *Record Breakers* on BBC1 to establish a world record pit-stop time of 4.8 seconds for the changing of all four wheels.

ABOVE The Brabham pit crew prepares the BT52B in the pits at Kyalami.
(John Townsend)

Chapter Five

The driver's view

In this chapter the BT52's regular drivers, Nelson Piquet and Riccardo Patrese, pass on their recollections of driving the car, and a surprisingly large number of other drivers also provide contributions.

As one of the top teams of the day, Brabham invited a great many up-and-coming drivers to test the BT52 with a view to joining the team if they were good enough – and one old hand also had a go in the car. So it was that two of motor racing's most legendary names – Stirling Moss and Ayrton Senna – both had outings in a BT52.

OPPOSITE After over 20 years away from F1, Sir Stirling Moss returned to the cockpit of an F1 car when he tested the Brabham BT52. *(John Townsend)*

Nelson Piquet

Nelson Piquet Souto Maior gave up a potential career in tennis to start motor racing, going on to win the Brazilian national karting title in 1971 and 1972. After winning the national Formula Vee title in 1976 he headed to Europe.

Victory in the 1978 BP Formula 3 Championship led to his Formula 1 début with Ensign and further outings in a BS Fabrications McLaren. For 1979 he signed for Brabham and became the *de facto* team leader when Niki Lauda retired mid-season.

He scored the first of his 23 grand prix wins at Long Beach in 1980 and challenged for the title that year. He took the first of his three World Championship titles in 1981. After that spell of success, his first impressions of the BT52 were less than positive.

'The rules changed a lot from the BT49 to the BT52,' Piquet says. 'We had much less downforce on the BT52 but we had a lot more power with the turbo engine. The big difference was we had to use such a big rear wing to compensate the power and not lose the downforce and save the tyres.'

The late arrival of the BT52 meant that neither Piquet nor Riccardo Patrese had the full winter test programme they would have been expecting. Despite this, the performance of the car during its first public outing in Rio ahead of the season-opening Brazilian Grand Prix gave them reasons to be optimistic, although the lack of development miles the car had covered meant that there were obvious concerns about whether it would be able to make the finish, especially given the blistering Brazilian heat.

Of course the concerns about the reliability ahead of Rio were ill-founded as Piquet dominated the race. It was a doubly sweet win for him: not only was it a home win in front of a passionate and vocal partisan crowd, but it also atoned for the disappointment of 1982, when he was disqualified from victory after his car was adjudged to be underweight.

'It was difficult because we'd done a lot of tests in the winter time [with the unraced BT51] when it was cold, but in Brazil it was very hot,' Piquet says. 'The difference in power was very big and I managed to make the engine survive to the very end and we won.'

Testing during the season was carried out by both drivers. While there were developments made on the car, not least the B-spec version that was introduced for the British Grand Prix in July, most testing work concentrated on assessing modifications made to BMW's M12/13 engine.

'In 1983 we developed the engine more than the chassis,' Piquet confirms, 'but Gordon was very clever and the car was already born very good. We had a lot of experience from the previous car [BT50] and the monocoque was very rigid but with a very big fuel tank. But as soon as we started to do the fuel stop and we started to use much less fuel, we were able to make the tyres survive better. This was much better after we started to warm the tyres ahead of the tyre change.'

Although the young drivers who were given the opportunity to test the car when Piquet and Patrese were elsewhere all spoke of their difficulties adapting to its demands, as described later in this chapter, Piquet claims that the car was easy to drive compared with the BT50 of 1982.

'We had a lot of turbo lag in 1982 and the beginning of 1983. But with the development through the year, and the increase in power in the low part of the engine with the new turbocharger, after that it was quite easy to win the races and to win the World Championship.

'The car was not fragile but the engine was very delicate. To have an engine with so much more power you had to use it very cleverly. From the beginning I understood that to win the championship and to finish all the races we could not go to the limit all the time. We had to

LEFT Two championships in three seasons made Piquet the dominant driver of the early 1980s. *(John Townsend)*

be careful with the over-revving, be careful with the gearbox, because the engine was so strong through the gearbox. And that was the reason I was successful and Riccardo was breaking engines and gearboxes.'

After seven seasons with Brabham, Piquet left at the end of 1985 to go to Williams as Nigel Mansell's team-mate in a mega-money

LEFT Piquet scored the final race win for Brabham in 1985.

(John Townsend)

RIGHT Despite
his reputation as a
practical joker, Piquet
was respected as a
test driver.
(John Townsend)

FAR RIGHT Piquet's
iconic helmet design
is still used by son
Nelson Piquet Jr today.
(John Townsend)

deal, and he won his third World Championship title with his new team in 1987. During his time with Williams, Piquet came to be vilified by the British press, and partly brought this upon himself with his disparaging comments about Mansell's wife. At Brabham, however, he was always well liked and highly regarded.

'Nelson was demanding but good fun,' says Harvey Spencer, who engineered the spare car. 'He put his work in.'

'I used to get on very well with him,' says David North. 'I really liked him. He was a great character. He was a good driver, full stop. In the early days, when he was really keen, I used to do the wind-tunnel testing, and sometimes he used to come down and help out. He had a big Mercedes saloon and a couple of times we loaded up the wind-tunnel model in his Merc and drove down to Southampton University together.'

'A nice, strange and interesting guy,' surmises Pierre Dupasquier of Michelin. 'He was a good performer and serious as far as understanding what comes from tyres and what comes from the car. We were lucky that we worked with 10 or 15 of the best drivers in the world, so I never question drivers. I know they work absolutely professionally. But each had their own personality. His times were dependable, sometimes his comments were

blunt – "That's a shit tyre!" – but joking aside he was very interesting and professional.'

After spells at Lotus and Benetton, Piquet retired at the end of 1991, having competed in 204 grands prix. The following year he attempted to make his Indy 500 début but suffered a leg-shattering accident in practice. He recovered and took the start the following year but has suffered leg pain ever since.

His son Nelson Piquet Jr won the British Formula 3 title in 2004 and was the inaugural Formula E champion in 2015.

Riccardo Patrese

When Riccardo Patrese retired at the end of the 1993 Formula 1 season it was after a then record 256 starts covering stints at Shadow, Arrows, Brabham, Alfa Romeo, Williams and Benetton. He took six wins. Prior to Formula 1 he had been a karting champion and won the European Formula 3 Championship in 1976.

'My first impression was that the driving position was very forward,' Patrese recalls of the BT52. 'We were also sitting very high and because of that it felt a little bit strange in the beginning, but then I got used to this position. There were no electronics controlling traction on the engine and so on, so it was a complicated car to drive, but in those days that was what we had.'

Patrese retired from the first race, at Rio, with a broken exhaust, and setbacks plagued him for the whole year as he went on to finish only three of the 15 races. The most disappointing retirement came at Imola, where he crashed just moments after taking the lead in his home grand prix. He feels this was a pivotal moment in his season.

'My key point was unfortunately Imola where I crashed at *Aqua Minerali*. If it hadn't been for that problem I could win the grand prix and go and fight for the championship. But because of that I think all the attention became around Nelson.

'Because we didn't have a super-reliable engine, I think they decided to always give to me new things to try before giving them to Nelson, and unfortunately my car broke down many times that year. I think that mainly it was because they wanted to have development in one car and the other to be reliable and to go for points, and in fact this strategy worked very well because at the end of the day we won the championship with Nelson.

'The testing was split equally between the two drivers. In those days when you went testing you had a lot of things to do so we were working together to evaluate all the things we

had. We both had to work hard as we didn't have any test driver.

'They were trying new things in my car, so I was testing things within grands prix, while Nelson always had the safer things and because of this many times my car broke down that year – apart of course from the last grand prix that year when I had exactly the same specification as Nelson.

RIGHT Patrese won
two races during his
first spell with the
Brabham team.
(John Townsend)

BELOW Ecclestone
gives Patrese some
advice in 1983.
(John Townsend)

'That was the strategy of the team and I was a driver of the Brabham team and I had to do my job, so I knew that I could have problems but I accepted what they wanted me to do. When you know what's going on and you know that you're doing your job well, you're working for a team you have to do what is the best for the team, so at the end that was OK.'

As discussed in Chapter Four, the BT52 was designed to have a limited range of set-up options, but neither driver found this to be an issue. This was demonstrated by the car's performance at two particular tracks: the drivers were (almost) as competitive at Monaco, where Piquet was second, as they were at Monza, despite these circuits requiring the almost polar opposite in terms of car set-up.

'It was true that there wasn't much that you could change,' confirms Patrese. 'I think that the main thing was the big wings front and rear, so we produced a lot of downforce with the wings. And of course the power of the BMW engine. Plus we had really good grip with the Michelin tyres. So with big wings, a lot of power and Michelin tyres it made the right mixture to have a quick car and a winning car. There wasn't much to do really.

'Because of the characteristics of the engine, because of the power and the responsiveness not being very good, when we had long straights and quick corners the car was better suited. But I think even in Monte Carlo with the small turbo and the special engine for that kind of circuit, we were not so bad.'

During the final three races of the season, Piquet won twice and was on course for a hat-trick in South Africa when he was made aware that Alain Prost and René Arnoux had retired. Knowing he just needed three points for the championship, he backed off. This allowed Patrese to come through to win, but this was not some preordained agreement – it was simply a pragmatic decision in order to ensure that the title was secured.

'It was a World Champion car, so you have to say it was a fantastic car,' Patrese concludes. 'When you have a car that wins the World Championship you can always say it was a beautiful car. But it was not an easy car to drive because of the characteristic of the engine – it was very strong but not very gentle.'

At the end of the 1983 season Patrese moved to Alfa Romeo, where he spent two seasons before returning to Brabham alongside fellow Italian Elio de Angelis, but by this time the team's glory days were over. His Formula 1 career, however, was resurrected when he replaced Piquet as Nigel Mansell's team-mate at Williams, where he remained for five seasons.

During his Formula 1 career Patrese also raced factory Lancia sports cars, while after Formula 1 he returned to Le Mans with Nissan, drove a factory Ford Mondeo in the German Super Touring series, and took part in the short-lived Grand Prix Masters series.

Stirling Moss

A full 21 years after his horrific crash at Goodwood brought a premature end to his Formula 1 career, Stirling Moss was invited to drive a Brabham BT52 at Brands Hatch on the shorter Indy version of the track.

'Stirling worked closely with us on our end-of-season videos,' recalls Herbie Blash. 'We produced everything at the Brabham factory and then Stirling would come along and add a commentary for us. He's obviously a great friend of Bernie's as they go back to when they first started racing.

BELOW On a beautiful sunny day at Brands, Stirling Moss tried a turbocharged F1 car for the first time. *(John Townsend)*

ABOVE **Moss and Brabham team manager Herbie Blash at Brands.** *(John Townsend)*

'I can't remember whether it was Bernie or me who asked Stirling if he would like to try the car. It wasn't a big publicity stunt at all. It was lovely to see and it was lovely for Stirling to test what was in those days such an up-to-date, modern race car.'

Moss arrived at the track with his blue Dunlop overalls, Herbert Johnson crash hat and goggles.

'The Brabham boys were a bit taken aback,' says Moss in his book *Stirling Moss: My Racing Life*, co-written with Simon Taylor, 'but I told

them that was how I'd always dressed to drive a racing car and I wasn't about to change now. I had special dispensation from the FIA, which meant I could run with my open-face helmet and still wear silk overalls, not the big, clumsy things they were wearing then. Only Sir Jack Brabham and I were allowed to do that.'

After a series of tracking laps behind a camera car, Moss was let loose in the flame-spitting racer.

'Until you really tried to approach the limit the car was quite easy to drive with the huge grip from those big slicks. But the power was simply unbelievable: when the turbo came in at around 8,000rpm it made the whole car feel like it was going into orbit. I was enjoying myself so much that I stayed out a long time, and after 40 laps I spun at what we used to call Kidney Bend. But I carried on, and in all I did 60 laps, getting down to a best of 46.6 seconds. They told me Nigel Mansell had done a test there a few weeks before and done a 41.1 seconds, so I reckoned that 5.5 seconds off the pace wasn't too bad in a completely strange type of car against somebody who drove one all the time.

'It was quite an eye-opening experience as it obviously had much more power than anything I was used to. The experience really did impress me immensely.'

Three other drivers were present for testing

RIGHT **Complete with open-faced helmet and goggles, Moss prepares to hit the track.** *(John Townsend)*

that day and comparison with their times is interesting: Pierluigi Martini set the pace with a lap of 41.75 seconds, while Davy Jones and Ivan Capelli both recorded best times of 43.7 seconds.

Capelli recalls being impressed by the level of commitment Moss showed: 'He was really pushing in the car, not just cruising for the footage – he was really testing the car. He was in his 50s at the time but he was at full throttle when he could. I was amazed by the fact that he was really pushing, but, no, he wasn't quicker than me! But you could see that he was taking it seriously and enjoying it.'

Ivan Capelli

Ivan Capelli's test at Brands Hatch in 1983 came about through his father's connections with Parmalat – the Italian food producer that was the main sponsor of the team. Capelli senior was a cameraman who had been making TV commercials for Parmalat and the company was helping to sponsor his son in Italian Formula 3 that season.

'When I arrived at the Brabham factory together with Pierluigi Martini, we were introduced to Gordon Murray,' Capelli remembers. 'We went into his office and the person who introduced us said, "This is Ivan Capelli and Pierluigi Martini, the two Italian drivers." Gordon was probably already thinking about the lowline car: when he saw that Pierluigi was so small, he didn't talk to me at all! He was just looking at Pierluigi and probably designing the perfect car around him – the smallest driver they could have!

'We had a very English-style test, let's put it like that. We had 20 laps each, ten laps with used tyres and ten laps with new tyres for both of us. Herbie Blash was there as team manager. I didn't know the Brands Hatch circuit and obviously I didn't know the car because it was the first time I had driven a Formula 1 car. After the first ten laps I said to myself, "Why am I here driving this powerful car?" It was a very big shock moving from Formula 3 to an engine with nearly 1,000bhp.

'Although it was difficult at first, I was able to feel a bit better in the cockpit by the end of the 20 laps. But the turbo engines in 1983 were

very difficult to manage – you needed at least 100 laps to start to understand how it worked. I wasn't really able to judge the car because I couldn't go at the limit. I just understood that the car was probably the best package that was in Formula 1 at that time. We had the Michelin tyres as well that were working quite well, particularly when I had the new set.'

After a stellar career in Formula 3, which included the Italian and European championships, Capelli eventually made his Formula 1 début for Tyrrell in 1985 and went on to start 93 races for AGS, March/Leyton House, Ferrari and Jordan. After leaving Formula 1 he raced touring cars for Nissan, but he has remained a regular presence in the Formula 1 paddock due to his TV work for Rai in Italy.

Davy Jones

Davy Jones, who was the only driver other than Ayrton Senna and Martin Brundle to win a British Formula 3 race during 1983, also attended the Brands Hatch test alongside Capelli and Martini. Aged only 19 at the time, he owed his test to a conversation with Bernie Ecclestone while at Silverstone for the British Grand Prix.

'I was talking with Bernie about being an American in Europe and he invited me to test the car at Brands Hatch,' Jones says. 'From what I recall, Bernie was in conversation with Del Monte, an American company, and putting me in the car was an opportunity that might have leveraged the discussion, saying, "Look, we have a young American driver testing the car".'

It was Jones's first experience of a turbo car, let alone such a powerful one, and he feels that he never really got to grips with the driving style required.

'I remember going out in it and just trying to get a feel for when the power came in. You try to brake in a nice straight line, then go into the corner and go for the accelerator – but when you went for the accelerator there was no power. There was nothing – there was nobody home! And then all of a sudden it was like a light switch and it just came on all at once. So then you'd come off the throttle and feed it back in.

'I remember clearly Herbie Blash saying to me that Nelson was really able to monitor

ABOVE **Murray speaks to Senna after his first run in the BT52B.**
(John Townsend)

BELOW **Senna analyses the data following his run at Paul Ricard.**
(John Townsend)

when the boost came up and was able to back off the throttle and then go back onto it to modulate the power band. There was just so much turbo lag that for me, jumping from a Formula 3 car to a Formula 1 car, that instantaneous power was quite an awakening when it came. It was enough of an awakening for me to realise that I needed to do another year of Formula 3!'

Although his Formula 1 aspirations were never fulfilled, Jones enjoyed success in sports cars and won the 1996 Le Mans 24 Hours for Reinhold Joest's team. However, a terrible accident at the Walt Disney World Speedway in 1997 left him with a broken neck – but he recovered well enough to race on for a while. Nowadays he is an advisor to buyers of high-performance road cars.

Ayrton Senna

When Riccardo Patrese decided to go to Alfa Romeo, having apparently asked for more money than Bernie was prepared to offer, the search was on for a new number two

for 1984. At Paul Ricard at the end of 1983 there was another batch of young hopefuls who were given their opportunity. Foremost among them was the new British Formula 3 champion, Ayrton Senna, who had made his Formula 1 test début for Williams a few months earlier, and had recently also tried the Toleman.

ABOVE Senna heads out for another run at Paul Ricard. *(John Townsend)*

BELOW Senna impressed the team, but his times were well off Piquet's, contrary to common belief. *(John Townsend)*

On a cold Monday morning, Piquet went out first to set up the car and establish a benchmark time. The new World Champion recorded a lap of 1m 05.9s, according to the *Autosport* report of the test. Despite a spin, Senna then recorded a best lap of 1m 07.9s, which was equalled by Pierluigi Martini, who was having his second run in the car, his first having been at Brands Hatch.

Senna's time in the car impressed everybody at Brabham, but any hopes the team had of acquiring his services were thwarted when Piquet spoke to Calisto Tanzi, CEO of Parmalat, and told him that he would go elsewhere if Senna was taken on.

At the Paul Ricard test Piquet then turned to a modified version of the BT52B in which he set a new 'flat-bottom' lap record in 1m 02.6s.

Mauro Baldi

Mauro Baldi's switch from rallying to circuit racing early in his career led to a stellar stint in Formula 3, which culminated with the 1981 European title. This led to a Formula 1

race seat with Arrows in 1982. He switched to Alfa Romeo for 1983, but lost out when Benetton came on board as the title sponsor for 1984.

Baldi set the fastest time at the Paul Ricard test. Owing to his two years in Formula 1, and particularly his familiarity with Alfa's new V8 turbo engine, he was by far the most experienced driver at the test, and he just eclipsed Senna's time.

'I was invited by Nelson and the Olivetti people, because Brabham was looking for a second driver,' says Baldi. 'Like all the other drivers I think I had 10 or 15 laps, I think in two stints, so maybe 20 laps altogether. For sure, the BMW engine was more powerful than the Alfa at the top end. I remember the car had quite a lot of understeer, but that was no problem for me because I liked understeering cars, so I got used to it quite quickly. I was surprised by the amount of understeer – maybe Nelson liked to drive the car like this.

'I was also surprised by the set-up of the car. I was expecting it to be much more efficient and balanced than the Alfa, but the Alfa was more balanced. The Alfa was a good car, very well balanced, but there was a lack of power.'

Despite setting the pace, Baldi never heard anything further from the team, and eventually he signed for the underfunded Spirit team for the 1984 season.

ABOVE Baldi was impressed by the BMW power, but less complimentary about the Brabham chassis.
(John Townsend)

'Bernie was looking for money. He didn't like to pay drivers and I wanted to be paid, even if it wasn't a lot! I would have gone with pleasure to be the second driver to Nelson Piquet and it would have been a great opportunity after my season with Alfa, because their engine was blowing up all of the time and with the BT52 I was sure I could do some good results.'

Driving for the Spirit team brought little in the way of results, and when Toleman absorbed the team in early 1985 Baldi left Formula 1. A successful career in sports cars followed, with victory in the 1990 FIA World Sports-Prototype Championship and winning the 1994 Le Mans 24 Hours the high points.

LEFT Baldi reckoned the Alfa Romeo chassis was a match for the Brabham's after his test in 1983.
(John Townsend)

ABOVE **Martini equalled Senna's times in his Brabham test at Paul Ricard.**
(John Townsend)

Pierluigi Martini

Pierluigi Martini was also at the Paul Ricard test and, having previously driven the BT52 at Brands Hatch, he was a little more prepared for it than the other young hopefuls under assessment there.

'The car was good,' remembers Martini. 'There was a lot of understeer because the rear downforce was huge with the turbo engine, but in the fast corners it was very well balanced.

'At the time Senna had just won the British Formula 3 Championship and I was winning the European Formula 3 Championship, so we

RIGHT **It was Martini's second test for Brabham, having previously had a run at Brands Hatch.**
(John Townsend)

considered ourselves to be rivals – although later on the relationship changed and we became good friends. He was very reserved and focused at that test, and quite distant – this is the only thing I remember really. The following day we headed to Macau for the Formula 3 Grand Prix: he won the race and I retired quite early in a tangle with Martin Brundle.'

When Toleman suspended Senna for breach of contract ahead of the 1984 Italian Grand Prix, Martini stepped in to make the first of 124 Formula 1 starts. Most were for the Minardi team, but he also had a spell at Scuderia Italia.

After he left Formula 1 at the end of 1995 he raced sports cars for Porsche and BMW before returning to single-seaters for Grand Prix Masters. He most recently raced a Cadillac in the Superstars touring car series.

Roberto Guerrero

Another up-and-coming driver present at the Paul Ricard test was Colombian driver Roberto Guerrero, who was able to slot in the opportunity ahead of his drive alongside Senna for Eddie Jordan's team in the Macau Grand Prix the following weekend. Guerrero was familiar with Cosworth DFV power as he had raced in Formula 1 during 1982 for Ensign and 1983 for Theodore, where he never managed

to trouble the score sheets but nevertheless showed up well against team-mate Johnny Cecotto, and he did qualify an impressive 11th at Detroit.

'I had never really driven a turbocharged car before – and talk about a turbo car!' he exclaims. 'The turbo lag was so unbelievably

ABOVE Piquet and Senna in attendance as Guerrero gets ready for his test run.
(John Townsend)

LEFT After two seasons in F1, Guerrero gives his feedback on the BT52 to Murray.
(John Townsend)

bad that I still have no idea how Nelson Piquet was able to drive the car. It was hard enough to drive at a place like Paul Ricard, so I can't imagine what it must have been like at Monaco or Detroit. I kept on bringing the car in saying, "There's something wrong! There's no way that this is normal." I remember on the back straightaway how it would kick you up the behind. It was just unbelievable how fast it went. You would put your foot on the gas and count 1–2–3 and then, *boom*, 800bhp all of a sudden. Wow!'

Guerrero's best time was 1m 08.6s. He then flew with Senna to Macau, where he qualified on the front row next to the Brazilian and went on to finish behind him in the race.

'The test obviously wasn't very successful for me,' Guerrero admits. 'I didn't do super well as I clearly thought there was something wrong with that car. The funny thing is that both Senna and myself were leaving that evening for the Formula 3 race in Macau, so it was a bit of a rush to do the test and then run to the airport and get to Macau for official practice, which started the next day. I was already a Formula 1 driver and I was put together with these little Formula 3 guys. Senna qualified on pole and I was second, and he won the race and I was second – and I remember being kind of mad that a Formula 3 driver beat me. But as it happened I'm not so mad anymore as he ended up being one of the most talented drivers ever. It was pretty cool.'

Guerrero never raced in Formula 1 again. Instead he moved to the US Champ Car scene for 1984 and became that year's Indy 500 Rookie of the Year. A huge crash at Indy in 1987 left him in a coma for 17 days but he recovered and raced on until 1996. A highlight was his pole position for the 1992 Indy 500 – the event where Piquet sustained career-ending injuries in qualifying.

BELOW Guerrero was convinced there was a problem with the car the turbo-lag was so bad. *(John Townsend)*

LEFT Fabi had a brief
run in the BT52 before
its successor the BT53
(pictured) took over
for the 1984 season.
*(Sutton Motorsport
Images)*

Teo Fabi

Brabham's number-two seat for 1984 was
eventually awarded to the Fabi brothers,
Teo and Corrado.

Teodorico Fabi was a star of European
Formula Ford before enjoying success in
Formula 3 and Formula 2. This led to a Formula
1 début with Toleman in 1982, but it was his
stunning rookie performances in CART that
brought him to the attention of Brabham.

He spent 1983 racing in the US in Champ
Cars, where he had proved to be an impressive
rookie for the Forsythe team, finishing second
in the championship and taking four wins. As
a result, for 1984 he ran a dual campaign in
both Formula 1 and Champ Car. When there
was a clash between the two, Corrado, who
had raced for Osella in Formula 1 during 1983,
would step in.

'Teo looked like someone special with his
American showing,' says Herbie Blash. 'And he
was nice and small and light, and, of course,
he was Italian, which kept our sponsors happy.
And then his brother Corrado had won the
1982 Formula 2 Championship and in those
days if you were the Formula 2 champion you
were a star in the making. So Bernie got two
cheap drivers with great potential.'

Teo Fabi initially tested the BT52 while Gordon
Murray worked on finishing off the BT53, the car
the team would campaign throughout 1984. Teo's
running took place mainly at Kyalami in South
Africa, but he says he never really had a chance
to fully assess the BT52's ability.

'I did a few tests, but not very much really,'
he recalls. 'Most of the time my car was fitted
with data-logging equipment so it was quite
heavy, and it was all put on the back of the
car so the balance wasn't really that good.
And most of the time I did long runs to check
temperatures so I never really tried the car in
race performance.'

Aside from his place on the podium at
Detroit, where Piquet won, Fabi's 1984 season
failed to live up to expectations, but he has no
regrets about how it panned out.

'Brabham was probably the best team at
the time and I enjoyed working with Bernie. We
are still in touch and I'm very grateful for the
opportunity he gave me. Unfortunately, after my
year Parmalat stopped sponsoring the team
and he had to change driver.'

Teo returned to Toleman in 1985 and stayed
there when the team morphed into Benetton.
Despite recording three pole positions, he
never led a race lap. For 1988 he returned to
CART with Porsche. Alongside his single-seater
career he enjoyed great success in sports cars,
including winning the FIA Sportscar World
Championship in 1991. He retired from racing
at the end of 1996.

Chapter Six

The team's view

─────●─────

Even by the standards of 1980s F1, Brabham was a small team, with only around 30–40 people making up the entire workforce. Even so, within that tightly-knit group was an enormous breadth of talent, and even today some of the most influential people in Formula 1 can trace their roots back to the Chessington factory in Surrey. In this chapter, we hear their thoughts on the BT52.

OPPOSITE The Brabham team mastered pit stops, and could change all four wheels and tyres, and refuel, in under 10 seconds. *(Sutton Motorsport Images)*

Compared with the Formula 1 teams of today, which operate out of enormous space-age factories with departments staffed by hundreds of people, the Brabham team of the early 1980s was tiny. Actually, even compared with the contemporary powerhouse factory teams of Ferrari and Renault, and even 'privateer' McLaren and Williams, it was still a small outfit.

But Brabham was staffed with some brilliant and resourceful people, and the team developed a reputation for not just working hard but playing hard too. The results speak for themselves.

In the period from the termination of the Alfa Romeo engine deal (midway through the 1979 season) up until the radical but flawed BT55 'lie-down' car (introduced for the 1986 season), Brabham took two drivers' World Championship titles and scored 292 points, and achieved 15 wins, 19 pole positions and 15 fastest laps.

LEFT The partnership with BMW had a rocky start, but ultimately delivered.
(John Townsend)

This was a remarkable achievement for a team of around 35 people. The fact that the team was so small makes what happened in 1983 – the construction of two completely new cars featuring ground-breaking new concepts like refuelling and the race rear end – even more impressive.

'I loved the fact that we were giant-killers,' smiles Gordon Murray. 'Our budget compared with Ferrari, Renault, McLaren and even Williams was peanuts really, and we'd go out there and beat them. We had a very good team of people.

'It's always a bonus when you have a pretty car win the championship. Bernie of course loved it. He loves things to look right and look nice. When I first showed Bernie a drawing of the BT52 and we started making the wooden pattern for the moulds, he absolutely loved it.

LEFT Murray inspects Piquet's car before he heads out on track.
(John Townsend)

'What upset him, though, was that I was trying to get the nose absolutely clear, but when you're doing everything in such a rush you always have cock-ups – and there was a cock-up with the cast-magnesium rockers. They broke through the top skin so at the last minute I had to go back to the pattern.

'Our pattern maker was Mike Reid, a fantastic guy but with a massive temper, so I had to creep in very quietly and ask if he wouldn't mind redoing the nose. And that's where the little bumps come from. Aerodynamically they don't make any difference at all as they are so smooth.'

Murray's skills extended way past simply designing the car. He took an interest in all aspects of the car's performance, which was very much appreciated by Pierre Dupasquier at Michelin.

'Gordon is smart,' Dupasquier states. 'We worked together on the McLaren F1 too. In my opinion he was the best engineer I worked with for two reasons: his competence and knowledge, and the way he relates with people, listening to what they are saying.'

Dupasquier's observations were exemplified in the concept of the car. In those days Murray used to engineer the car too and he was able to understand things from an engineer's perspective. This is one of the reasons why the BT52 was built the way it was, with the front and rear removable in single pieces. This piece of engineering inspiration may not have made the cars any faster, but it made them much easier and, more importantly, quicker to work on.

By reducing the hours the mechanics had to work, Murray's thinking also reduced their fatigue and therefore the potential for small but crucial mistakes to be made through lack of concentration. And he was demonstrably proved right in South Africa. While the challenge from Renault and Ferrari wilted under the strain, when it mattered both Brabhams ran faultlessly.

'It was a fabulous car,' says chief mechanic Charlie Whiting. 'We were absolutely amazed when we first saw it. With the flat-bottom rule, which came out for 1983, the idea was to get as much weight backwards as you possibly

ABOVE **The building has now been turned into a series of individual industrial units.** (*John Townsend*)

LEFT **The team had its only windtunnel and autoclave at Chessington.** (*John Townsend*)

could, and this was a completely unique design – and it remains to this day a unique design. It was so amazing how he did it: attaching the intercooler, the radiators, the oil coolers all to the back of the car like that rearwards of the rear bulkhead of the chassis.

'We didn't realise this at the time, but the design of the car gave rise to the reliability we were able to achieve with it. We were literally able to remove the whole back end of the car and replace it with a new one that we had prepared ready for the race – new engine, new gearbox, new intercoolers. Everything new, bang, on it went. Two hours after qualifying

we were ready for the race. It was remarkable in that respect. I don't think it has ever been copied really.'

Under Whiting's marshalling, the free time that the detachable rear end created was put to full use. Everything that could be stripped down and rebuilt at the track was done.

'It was one of those almost perfect years,' recalls Roly Vincini, who worked on the transmission and was part of the pit-stop crew. 'I've been in motorsport most of my life, but that was still the best time. Because of the organisation within the team and the amount of fun we had.

'Charlie Whiting was the superstar of the team. But for him we wouldn't have won the championship. The way he floor-managed the team, the way he managed the preparations prior to and after the event – the whole thing was very well run.'

Unless the car had been involved in a crash, the Brabham boys were usually able to pack up and leave the circuit early in the evenings during a race weekend. This was hours before their rivals, and they used this to their advantage by making sure the other teams were fully aware that they had knocked off for the night.

'It was amazing how we got ourselves organised for that season,' adds Whiting. 'And

that gave us not only a physical advantage but also a significant psychological advantage. By four or five o'clock on a Saturday we were covering up the car ready for Sunday – that must have annoyed Renault big-time!'

Of course, much of this extra time was put to good use in the 'boozer', where the fantastic camaraderie of the Brabham team was forged. The impact the members of that team have had on Formula 1 since has been profound.

'When I look at Formula 1 now,' says team manager Herbie Blash, 'the Red Bull team is how I would have liked to see Brabham today. Red Bull is a close-knit team, they have the music going and they really gel together – and that's how it was at Brabham.'

After selling Brabham, Bernie Ecclestone put all his efforts into running FOCA and ultimately the whole of Formula 1. Murray departed for McLaren where he produced the MP4/4, which won 15 of 16 races in 1988. He also helped to get McLaren Cars off the ground, creating the legendary F1 road car.

Whiting went on to become Formula 1 race director and safety delegate. Herbie Blash remained at Brabham even after Ecclestone sold up and restored a number of Brabham chassis through Yamaha's Activa Technology business, which he ran. Since 1995 he's been the deputy race director of Formula 1 as well as maintaining his role as Yamaha's sporting director, through which he still has close contact with Murray whose company is developing a city car with support from the Japanese firm.

Herbie Blash – team manager

Michael 'Herbie' Blash joined Brabham as team manager in 1973 having previously worked at Lotus and Frank Williams' Politoys team. When Bernie Ecclestone sold Brabham in 1988, Blash followed him to FOCA, but returned to the team in 1991 after joining Yamaha (then Brabham's engine partner) as its sporting director – a role he still performs to this day.

When Brabham folded, Yamaha-owned Activa Technologies took over its former base in Chessington and among its activities was the restoration of a number of the Brabhams in Ecclestone's private collection. Although Activa is no longer based at Chessington, the company continues to thrive and, indeed, is currently working with Gordon Murray Design on a Yamaha city-car concept.

In 1995 Blash joined the FIA as its Deputy Race Director, a post he has retained to this day.

Rupert Manwaring – deputy team manager

Rupert Manwaring started his career at Team Surtees before joining Brabham in 1978 to work as the stores co-ordinator. After leaving Brabham in 1984 he had a brief stint working for the Kraco CART team before returning to Formula 1 with the Haas Lola project in 1985.

A move to Team Lotus eventually took him to the position of team manager, a role he went on to perform at Tyrrell. He stayed with the

BELOW The Brabham race team celebrates Piquet's 1983 title triumph as he crosses the line in South Africa. *(John Townsend)*

Tyrrell team after it was bought out by BAR but then left to join Harvey Postlethwaite's stillborn Honda project.

After a stint as team manager at Minardi, Manwaring became managing director at Lola Cars, where he remained until it folded in 2012. He now works at Lotus Cars, where he is head of motorsport.

Charlie Whiting – chief mechanic

When Hesketh Racing folded in 1977, Charlie Whiting joined Brabham, where he stayed for the next decade. As chief mechanic, he played a key role in the World Championship title wins of 1981 and 1983.

When Brabham was sold in 1988, Whiting joined the FIA as its Technical Delegate. This role was expanded in 1997 to become the Race Director and Safety Delegate, which he remains to this day. He is famously seen on TV as the man who presses the button that turns the lights out to start Formula 1 races.

Bruce MacIntosh – number one mechanic – Nelson Piquet

Bruce MacIntosh's long and varied career started with the British Racing Partnership (BRP) and incorporated spells at Parnell Racing and Scuderia Serenissima before his fluent Italian took him to Brabham at the time of its partnership with Alfa Romeo.

He was chief mechanic but left Brabham for a spell with Alfa. When he returned to Brabham he was the number one mechanic on Piquet's car, working under Charlie Whiting.

MacIntosh teamed up with Gordon Murray to help him establish McLaren Cars, where he remained until 2004. In 2005 he joined the FIA to become the Technical Delegate for GP2, which expanded to include GP3 in 2009. Alongside his GP2/3 role, he still works at Gordon Murray Design.

Roly Vincini – gearbox technician

Having cut his teeth with the RAM team in British Formula 1, Roly Vincini joined Brabham in 1981. His main role was looking after the gearboxes on the championship-winning BT52.

He moved to Lotus in 1985 before spells with West Surrey Racing and Reynard. In 1991 he established P1 Engineering, which would go on to work with a host of successful junior single-seater teams before becoming, in 2002, an entrant in its own right in the British Formula 3 championship. P1 entered Formula Renault 3.5 in 2008, winning the title with Alx Danielsson and Giedo van der Garde.

Having beaten a recent bout of cancer, Vincini plans to return to team ownership.

BELOW Herbie (left) and Bernie work closely to this day through their roles at FOM and the FIA. (*John Townsend*)

parmalat parmalat
parmalat
FILA
MICHELIN
Santàl
parmalat
FILA
parmalat
Santàl
Castrol
AVON
BIOPOINT
24

Chapter Seven

The BT52 today

In total six BT52/52Bs were built. Two were destroyed, one was given to BMW, while the other three remain part of Bernie Ecclestone's private car collection. Two of the cars have been fully restored, one by BMW, the other for Ecclestone. In this chapter, we look at the process behind these restorations, and the track appearances these revived cars have made

OPPOSITE Chassis 1 at the 2015 Austrian Grand Prix, where it ran faultlessly in Piquet's hands. *(Author)*

In total six Brabham BT52s were built. Chassis numbers 1, 2, and 3 were standard BT52s, while chassis numbers 4, 5 and 6 were the BT52Bs that were introduced at the British Grand Prix and featured a longer wheelbase, revised engine installation and a longer 'smooth' nose.

Four of these six cars survive today. Bernie Ecclestone owns the three BT52Bs while the single remaining BT52, chassis number 1, belongs to BMW.

Chassis number 2 was written off in an accident on 31 August 1983 during a private Brabham test at Brands Hatch. Little is known about what actually happened and there are no contemporary accounts in the specialist press.

The fire that engulfed Piquet's car in the 1983 German Grand Prix destroyed chassis number 3. Fuel leaking from the fuel filter spilled over the hot exhausts and ignited spectacularly. Even though German fire marshals attended the scene very quickly, they were unable to stop the damage from being terminal.

At the end of 1983 Brabham tested a number of developments of the BT52 that were branded 'BT52C' and 'BT52D' by the press, but Gordon Murray denies that these monikers were ever officially used by the team. These cars featured developments of the sidepod design and cooling solutions that were used to test concepts that went on to inform the design of the BT53, which

the team entered for the 1984 season. These 'C' and 'D' cars were subsequently taken back to their original specification.

Restoration of BT52-1

By the time the 1984 season had rolled around and Brabham had moved on to the BT53, BT52-1 had been shipped off to Munich and pride of place in BMW's museum. And that was where it remained for the next 30 years.

In 2012 the decision was made that for the following year's 30th anniversary of BMW's only Formula 1 World Championship win, the car should be rebuilt and put through its paces in public once again. Although the BMW team of 1983 supplied engines to ATS and Arrows as well as to Brabham, it totalled just 63 people – and a significant number of this band of brothers was brought back together for the job of restoring BT52-1.

Once again Paul Rosche led the team, although he admits that, 30 years on, the project was a challenge.

'My old mechanics and I had forgotten many things so we needed a lot of time,' Rosche says. 'We couldn't find a lot of the old documents and we had many problems. It was an old engine we rebuilt and it was a normal rebuild, so on the engine itself we did

RIGHT The BMW Motorsport team that rebuilt BT52-1 for the 2013 Goodwood Festival of Speed. *(BMW)*

The whole car, engine and gearbox was stripped down and painstakingly rebuilt. *(BMW)*

not have many problems. But the set-up of the electronics, a very old type, was difficult – and some things we couldn't remember. We had the original ECU, not a new type, but it was working OK – it was our brains that were the problem!'

The project began in October 2012 with the target of having the car up and running in time for the Goodwood Festival of Speed in July 2013.

Working almost 24 hours a day, bit by bit the team put the car back together. Once it had been painstakingly reassembled, the honour of putting it through its paces was entrusted to Marc Surer, who had raced for Brabham during the 1985 season, and had been a BMW junior driver earlier in his career.

Running the restored BT52-1

After months of dedicated hard work, the car finally turned a wheel in anger when Surer slipped into the cockpit and drove it out onto BMW's Regensburg test track. The BMW Press Club documented the rebuild in a

ABOVE The team rebuilt an old M12/13 engine and BMW documented the entire process. *(BMW)*

LEFT Paul Rosche (second left) talks to his team ahead of the first run of the newly restored car. *(Dirk Daniel Mann/BMW)*

ABOVE Surer gets ready for his first ever run in a Brabham BT52.
(Dirk Daniel Mann/BMW)

ABOVE RIGHT Surer gives his feedback on the car to Rosche.
(Dirk Daniel Mann/BMW)

BELOW BMW assembled many of the original team for the rebuild.
(Dirk Daniel Mann/BMW)

short film, which is the source for the following interviews with Surer and the mechanics who worked on the car.

'It's certainly an incredible feeling when you experience that again,' said Surer. '900 PS [887bhp] in one go. You press the throttle, then nothing happens for one or two seconds, then it all comes together. Then the wheels spin, so in the lower gears you need to be gentle on the throttle and then when you're in fourth, fifth and sixth gear you can really go

ABOVE LEFT AND ABOVE Surer familiarises himself with the BT52's cockpit and controls before putting it to the test. *(Dirk Daniel Mann/BMW)*

CENTRE The team fits the last piece of bodywork as the car nears its first run in almost 30 years. *(BMW)*

LEFT Surer raced for Brabham in 1985, but had never previously driven a BT52. *(BMW)*

RIGHT AND BELOW
The starter is inserted
into the back of the
BT52 and the BMW
engine is fired into life.
(Dirk Daniel Mann/BMW)

flat out, but then sadly the straight is already
coming to an end!'

Seeing the car running again brought back
many memories for the mechanics, who were
understandably proud of their achievement.

'I have to say, we were all a bit sceptical,
thinking that some problems were bound
to crop up, as, after all, it had been a long
time since it was last running,' says Reiner
Dippelhofer, a BMW engine mechanic. 'But it
was surprisingly good, I've got to say. With no
problems, just as it should be.'

'I continue to be incredibly proud to have this
privilege of helping to work here again on this
engine, this car,' adds Raimund Kupferschmid,
another engine mechanic. 'And to be able
to get the vehicle going again with the old
workforce, the old colleagues and drivers from
that time, in tandem, of course, with our boss
Paul Rosche.'

**BELOW Surer makes his way out onto BMW's
Regensburg test track.** *(Dirk Daniel Mann/BMW)*

Norbert Knerr, the head of historic motorsport, paid tribute to the work the team had produced. 'Without the former colleagues, the experts from back then, I mean the people who were in Formula 1 at that time, this project would never have been possible. Because they're the only ones with the know-how and ability to help to restore the vehicle in this way and to rebuild it as it was back then. And the great thing about it is that there are people working with us on the project who were in Formula 1 back then and are now retired, as well as people still working at BMW today. And the close interaction and focused working towards a single result is the lovely part of the whole story.

'When we began restoring the BT52 it was clear to us that the car would throw up a few tricky problems, especially in relation to the chassis and bodywork. And it was clear to us very quickly too that things would only work out if we took on the help of former experts, who together with the engineers and mechanics still working here would get it cracked.'

With the car up and running, it was shipped over to England where it was reunited with Nelson Piquet. Interest in the car was understandably high, and after Piquet had signed a succession of autographs, the starting motor was slotted into the back of the gearbox, the engine was fired up, and he headed off to the assembly area. Eventually he was called forward to the start line. He lowered the visor on his familiar red and white helmet and the revs rose. He dropped the clutch and roared off, but this was not a competitive run. He gently guided the car up Lord March's driveway in front of over 70,000 enthusiasts and into the holding area at the top of the hill. Helmet off, he then received a fantastic ovation as he coasted back down the hill.

'I only drove the car up and down very slowly because that car is impossible to try to start on cold tyres and this kind of thing,' said Piquet. 'And I didn't want to destroy a beautiful, nice,

RIGHT Surer put the car through its paces and it ran without any issues. *(BMW)*

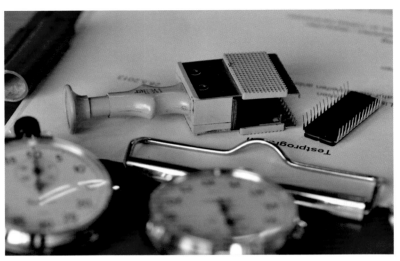

LEFT AND ABOVE
1983 ECU technology
is a world away from
today's, but fortunately
BMW still has the
old machine that
programs the chips.
(Dirk Daniel Mann/BMW)

LEFT BT52-1 is kept
on wet, treaded tyres
when it is being
transported. *(BMW)*

brand-new car. It was a nice show going up the hill without making any fuss or any stupid thing. All the noise, the gear-change, the difficulty to start, everything was exactly the same as I remembered. I had a good chance before Goodwood to go to the airport and do some starts and that was really nice, the engine is very, very powerful.'

With many of the ex-Brabham team present, there was a full reunion atmosphere, which carried on well after the hill was closed to the public for another year.

'We had a dinner,' remembers Gordon Murray. 'All the Brabham mechanics flew over, and Paul Rosche flew over. In fact Nelson went to pick up Rosche in his own jet. We had a lovely dinner down there and they all came back to my place and we had a lunch at my house. It was good.'

As BMW invested time and energy to get its BT52 up and running, the car has since become a fairly regular sight at gatherings of historic formula cars. In June 2015, for example, it formed part of a demonstration of classic turbo-era cars at the Austrian Grand Prix at the Red Bull Ring. Once again Piquet

ABOVE Piquet draws a crowd as he gets ready to run the BT52 during a demonstration of turbo-era cars at the 2015 Austrian Grand Prix. *(Author)*

BELOW Although Piquet took it easy, the fans were delighted to see the BT52 back in action at Goodwood in 2013. *(LAT)*

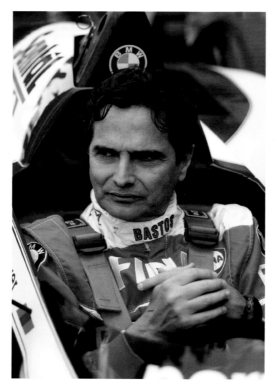

was called up to drive and once again the BT52 ran faultlessly as he wowed the crowds along with other greats, such as Alain Prost and Niki Lauda, from Formula 1's most powerful era.

Restoration of BT52B-4

As was the case with most redundant Brabhams at the time, the three BT52Bs were retained by Ecclestone and sent to be stored in Tom Wheatcroft's collection at Donington Park until his own storage facility at Biggin Hill was ready.

Ecclestone's private collection of cars includes at least one version of each Brabham built during his ownership of the team. One of each model has been restored to full working order, using original drawings as required. These restored specimens, however, are seldom run.

Chassis number 4 was the BT52B chosen for restoration. The process was undertaken early in the 2000s by Activa Technology, which was set up by Yamaha and was run by former Brabham team manager Herbie Blash. Activa was based in the old Brabham factory at Chessington and employed many ex-Brabham personnel. The company was established as a result of Yamaha's wish to have a small R&D

company and, when Brabham folded, Yamaha took over the facility. Activa carried out many restorations for Ecclestone, including a BT50 – the original turbo car.

Restoration work on the BT52B-4 began with the car being stripped down to the bare tub, which was then crack-tested. All individual components were also stripped down, checked, replaced or refurbished as required, and then reassembled. As there were still some old spares at the Chessington factory, in what old team personnel refer to as 'the dungeons', these were put to good use.

The suspension parts were crack-tested and then 'keyfossed', a process in which a black chemical coating is applied. This is appropriate for use on suspension items as traditional paint will inevitably chip off when pelted with stones and other track debris, while processes such as powder coating can disguise cracks, which could prove catastrophic if unnoticed. The suspension components – wishbones, uprights, spring/dampers units – were then realigned and remounted.

The engine was sent to Switzerland to be rebuilt by Heini Mader, who worked very closely with BMW in period. When BMW announced it was leaving Formula 1, Mader purchased the entire stock of parts, and continued to run the engines under the Megatron banner. Megatron supplied Ligier and Arrows in 1987, and Arrows again in 1988, after which turbos were banned.

Mader took the existing block and head of BT52 chassis number 4 and built up an as-new engine around them. One small but crucial change was made: in place of the old ECU a new engine-management system was designed and fitted into the original casing – a large box shaped like a biscuit tin.

As described in Chapter Four, the original ECU used a system called 'e-prom', which was commonplace at the time but presented two problems. The first problem was the one that occurred in period: once the various parameters – information such as fuel mixture and ignition rates – had been programmed onto the e-prom chip, nothing could be changed, so if a mistake has been made in the calculations or if a tweak was needed a new chip had to be burned. This led to the second problem: finding a machine that could burn e-prom chips!

Thus it was decided that a modern ECU would be created. The new ECU is about the size of a packet of cigarettes and fits easily inside the old 'biscuit tin', where the CDI unit and coil packs are also placed. The only visible difference is the presence at the back of the box of a small jack connection where a laptop can be plugged in and fine-tuning to the ECU can be done in minutes rather than hours.

The new ECU has made running the car much easier and has been programmed to include a warm-up routine. Previously, the task of getting the engine up to temperature was a meticulous one that required someone to patiently stand by monitoring temperature and oil pressure while gradually increasing the revs accordingly. Now the car sits in the garage and goes through the motions itself.

The other benefit of the new ECU is that the performance of the engine can be tailored for the circumstances. If the car is just going to potter around as the driver waves to the crowd, it can be adjusted so that it gives better response lower in the rev range. If the driver is going to gun it and give the fans a taste of 1980s turbo power, it can be set to best achieve that.

However, the BT52B is not eligible for racing. In order for a car to be certified for competition, evidence must be provided that crack-testing of all required elements of the car has been done. While all of this was carried out during the rebuild, the additional cost of getting the necessary certificate was not added in as there were no plans to enter the car for races.

Sadly the car barely runs at all these days. It was shipped to Bahrain in 2010 for the 60th anniversary celebration of the start of the Formula 1 World Championship, but did not run there because the fuel tank – the original ATL item – developed a leak, probably as a result of a crease in its rubber casing. After this failure it was decided that there was little point in going to the trouble and expense of repairing and refitting the original tank, so a much smaller, new, off-the-shelf tank was installed.

Because the restored BT52B-4 was only ever going to be used for demonstration runs, which by their very nature tend to be brief and with little or no use of full throttle, the car was only ever going to need enough fuel for a maximum of ten laps. Had such a small amount of fuel been used in the original tank, there would probably have been problems in any case with fuel pick-up.

At present the engine is set up to run at only 1.2 bar, which provides approximately 350bhp, because the boost adjuster was not working at the time the new ECU was programmed (by Track 'N' Road Powerformance in Essex). Although this modest output is more than enough for demonstration runs, it would leave the car looking a bit short of breath if it was run in anger.

Running the restored BT52B-4

Before every demonstration run the engine oil is changed and the clutch and brakes are bled. When the engine has been refilled with oil, the spark plugs are taken out and the engine is turned over by hand to help generate some oil pressure. Then the plugs are popped back in and checks are made to ensure that the fuel is picking up.

The fuel pumps on the BT52 had a reputation for being temperamental, and in particular for being prone to leaks. Bosch designed the pump for a Porsche turbo in 1974 and, despite being manufactured for only that year, it has been used by a variety of turbocharged engines. Bernie's team at Biggin Hill has created something of a stockpile of pumps, and they've also managed to find someone who has a tool that allows him to open up a pump and replace the troublesome leak-prone seal.

Once the fuel pressure is satisfactory, the ignition is turned on. The battery level is now checked and if everything is OK, the engine is fired up. Assuming it starts, which is usually the case, the engine is then allowed to run through its warm-up procedure as dictated by the ECU. With an engine rebuild costing around £60,000, warm-up needs to be done properly!

Although in its day the BT52 used chemically derived Toluene-based fuel (see Chapter Four), the introduction of the modern ECU means that the engine can easily be adapted to run on regular unleaded pump fuel or high-octane race fuel at the press of a button (or two).

Appendix 1

Specifications

Engine
BMW M12/13 in-line four-cylinder, longitudinally mounted
Capacity: 1,499cc
Bore and stroke: 89.2 x 60mm

Fuel
BASF

Lubricants
Castrol

Chassis
Monocoque: aluminium outer/carbonfibre inner

Suspension
Double wishbones, with pushrods operating coil spring/damper units front and rear
Front anti-roll bar

Transmission
Five/six-speed gearbox
Hewland internals with Brabham casing

Brakes
Girling carbon discs and pads front and rear

Tyres
Michelin: front 23/62x13; rear 40/66x13

Dimensions
BT52
Wheelbase: 2,860mm (113in)
Front track: 1,778mm (70.0in)
Rear track: 1,657mm (65.2in)

BT52B
Wheelbase: 2,845 mm (112in)
Front track: 1,753mm (69in)
Rear track: 1,626mm (64in)

Weight
540kg (1,190lb)

BELOW Piquet and Murray discuss how best to maximise the car's performance for the 1983 European GP.
(John Townsend)

Appendix 2

Brabham BT52 race history

Brazilian GP, Jacarepagua	13 March 1983	1st	Nelson Piquet	BT52-3
		Retired	Riccardo Patrese	BT52-2
US GP, Long Beach	27 March 1983	10th	Riccardo Patrese	BT52-2
		Retired	Nelson Piquet	BT52-3
Race of Champions, Brands Hatch	10 April 1983	Retired	Hector Rebaque	BT52-1
French GP, Paul Ricard	17 April 1983	2nd	Nelson Piquet	BT52-1
		Retired	Riccardo Patrese	BT52-2
San Marino GP, Imola	30 April 1983	Retired	Nelson Piquet	BT52-3
		Retired	Riccardo Patrese	BT52-4
Monaco GP, Monte Carlo	15 May 1983	2nd	Nelson Piquet	BT52-3
		Retired	Riccardo Patrese	BT52-4
Belgian GP, Spa-Francorchamps	22 May 1983	4th	Nelson Piquet	BT52-3
		Retired	Riccardo Patrese	BT52-4
US GP, Detroit	5 June 1983	4th	Nelson Piquet	BT52-3
		Retired	Riccardo Patrese	BT52-1
Canadian GP, Circuit Gilles Villeneuve	12 June 1983	Retired	Nelson Piquet	BT52-3
		Retired	Riccardo Patrese	BT52-1
British GP, Silverstone	16 July 1983	2nd	Nelson Piquet	BT52B-5
		Retired	Riccardo Patrese	BT52B-6
German GP, Hockenheim	7 August 1983	3rd	Riccardo Patrese	BT52B-6
		13th	Nelson Piquet	BT52B-3
Austrian GP, Österreichring	14 August 1983	3rd	Nelson Piquet	BT52B-5
		Retired	Riccardo Patrese	BT52B-6
Dutch GP, Zandvoort	28 August 1983	9th	Riccardo Patrese	BT52B-6
		Retired	Nelson Piquet	BT52B-5
Italian GP, Monza	11 September 1983	1st	Nelson Piquet	BT52B-5
		Retired	Riccardo Patrese	BT52B-6
European GP, Brands Hatch	25 September 1983	1st	Nelson Piquet	BT52B-5
		7th	Riccardo Patrese	BT52B-1
South African GP, Kyalami	15 October 1983	1st	Riccardo Patrese	BT52B-6
		3rd	Nelson Piquet	BT52B-5

Drivers' championship

1st	Nelson Piquet	59 points
9th	Riccardo Patrese	13 points

Constructors' championship

3rd	Brabham-BMW	72 points

Appendix 3

The rivals

The early 1980s was one of the most competitive eras in the history of Formula 1, despite the almost constant, often sweeping, rule changes, not to mention the extraordinary array of different technical solutions, most notably in the engines as four-cylinder, V6 and V8 turbos went up against V8, V12 and flat-12 normally aspirated versions, but also in chassis and aerodynamic terms. During the opening four seasons of the decade Brabham, Ferrari, Ligier, Lotus, McLaren, Renault, Tyrrell and Williams all won races, while Alfa Romeo and Arrows came close.

The rule changes for 1983 created a clean sheet of paper and an opportunity for the competitive order to be shuffled once more. As this book has documented, it was ultimately Gordon Murray's Brabham BT52 that prevailed, but 1983 was another super-competitive season. So here, to complete our coverage, is a look at the cars that Nelson Piquet and Brabham-BMW had to defeat to take the crown.

BELOW Tambay was a winner with Ferrari's 126C2B, with which the Maranello team started the season.
(John Townsend)

Ferrari
126C2/B & 126C3

Ferrari started the 1983 season as the reigning constructors' champions, but the 1982 season had been a tragic one for the Scuderia. The death of Gilles Villeneuve and the career-ending injuries suffered by Didier Pironi overshadowed the success that took place on track.

The 126C2 was designed by Harvey Postlethwaite, the British designer who had risen to prominence by creating Hesketh's race-winning 308 and the title-challenging Wolf WR1. It was his first car for the legendary Italian team and also their first to have a full monocoque made of aluminium honeycomb.

Ferrari had introduced its 120-degree 021 V6 turbo engine in 1981, but the 126CK, designed by Mauro Forghieri, was an overweight machine that Villeneuve christened 'the big red Cadillac' – but somehow dragged to memorable wins at Jarama and Monaco. But the twin-turbo engine was powerful and, by 1983, reliable too.

The design of turbo engines, especially twin-turbo ones, made it hard to extract the maximum potential of the ground-effect concept. In contrast to the compact Ford Cosworth DFV, whose V8 design neatly fitted around the underfloor wing designs, the placement of the turbos and intercoolers rather got in the way.

Thus the rule changes for 1983 had less of an impact on Ferrari than they did on many of the other teams on the grid, especially Brabham. So much of the 126C2 was carried over into the C3, which Postlethwaite also designed.

Ferrari started the season with a revised version of the 1982 car, dubbed 126C2/B. The new flat-bottom floor aside, the main difference from the previous car was in the engine installation, with radiators and intercoolers mounted further back, which made for shorter sidepods – the main visual difference between the cars.

The all-new C3 was introduced for the British Grand Prix. The most significant difference was the monocoque, where for the first time Ferrari used Kevlar and carbonfibre shells that were bonded together. As was the case with the C2, the suspension was double wishbones at both ends attached to pullrods. The brakes were cast-iron discs with aluminium calipers supplied by Brembo. Unlike most of its rivals, Ferrari used Goodyear's cross-ply tyres, having switched from Michelin after the 1981 season.

Even though Ferrari would adapt its car mid-season to follow Brabham's lead on in-race refuelling, the C3 had a 220-litre fuel tank, which was filled with Agip fuel.

The transmission featured a multi-plate clutch, a transverse gearbox that could run with five or six speeds depending on the circuit, and a ZF limited-slip friction-plate differential.

The 021 engine had its block and head made from alloy with aluminium wet liners. There were four valves per cylinder and two KKK turbochargers. A tie-up between Lucas and Ferrari produced the electronic direct fuel injection, while Magneti Marelli supplied the single-plug ignition system.

The C3 was the first car on the grid to sport winglets ahead of the rear wing on either side. These would soon be copied by most other teams.

In the driver line-up Patrick Tambay, who had joined the team in mid-1982 following Villeneuve's death, was joined by René Arnoux, whose relationship with Renault reached the point of no return in 1982 when he ignored team orders to win the French GP. Despite locking out the front row for race two at Long Beach (with Tambay on pole), it was a slow start to the season in terms of results at Ferrari.

All this changed in front of the passionate *Tifosi* at Imola for the San Marino GP. Arnoux started on pole, but it was Tambay who was in the right place to capitalise when Riccardo Patrese crashed out of the lead. Second place at Spa three weeks later thrust the Frenchman right into the title mix.

Arnoux had been third at Long Beach and San Marino, but out of the points elsewhere. However, victory in Canada kick-started his season. The arrival of the C3 also seemed to suit him better and wins in Germany and Holland and second places in Austria and Italy moved him to within just two points of the championship lead. However, a costly spin in the European GP at Brands and engine failure in the South African GP finale meant that Arnoux had to settle for third in the standings.

Tambay added further podium finishes in Canada, Britain and Holland (following home Arnoux for a Ferrari 1–2), but four no-scores over the final six races condemned him to fourth place in the points standings, although his and Arnoux's combined tally was enough for Ferrari to retain the constructors' championship by a convincing margin.

ABOVE Arnoux – seen here in the 126C3 – was a genuine title challenger, but retirement in the final race ended his hopes. *(John Townsend)*

Renault
RE30C & RE40

Like Ferrari, Renault was able to carry much of the RE30 from 1982 into the 1983 season. Indeed the RE30Cs with which it started the season were barely revised versions, with changes to the front and rear uprights the most significant modifications to the car aside from the flat floor as mandated by the new rules.

The chassis consisted of an aluminium honeycomb monocoque mounted to carbonfibre bulkheads. There was double wishbone suspension with pullrods at both ends while the Renault Gordini EFormula 1 90-degree V6 turbo engine was mounted longitudinally.

BELOW **The RE40 took Prost to the brink of the title, but he fell short when he retired from the South African finale.** *(John Townsend)*

This was the latest version of the motor that Renault introduced in 1977, which heralded the arrival of turbocharging to Formula 1. For 1983 the engine now featured revised electronic fuel injection, and had water injection that helped to keep the internal heat of the engine to a minimum.

Alain Prost only drove the RE30C for the season opener in Brazil, while new team-mate Eddie Cheever had to wait until round three in France to get his hands on the all-new RE40.

While visually very similar to the RE30C, the RE40 – designed by a team featuring Bernard Dudot, Michel Tetu and Jean-Claude Migeot – was the first Renault to feature a carbon composite monocoque. The carbon was produced by aerospace composites specialists Hurel-Dubois. Only the nose section crash box was made from aluminium.

Renault kept with KKK for the twin turbos on the EFormula 1 engine, while Elf continued to supply the fuel and Michelin the tyres as had been the case since 1977.

Despite there being no ground-effect benefit, Renault persevered with full-length sidepods

on the RE40. The team kept with the same suspension solution as used in the RE30, while the gearbox used Hewland internals in a bespoke Renault casing.

Prost finished outside the points in the RE30C in Brazil, while Cheever retired with turbo failure. Neither driver scored in Long Beach, as Prost gave the RE40 its début and Cheever brought the RE30's career to an end. However, for the next race – its home grand prix at Paul Ricard – Renault locked out the front row, with Prost on pole.

The Frenchman dominated the race, coming home half a minute ahead of Piquet in second place, while Cheever opened his Renault account with third. A run of four straight podiums for Prost, which culminated in victory in Belgium, moved him to the head of the points table.

Further wins in Britain and Austria made Prost the favourite to take the title heading into the final races. But three non-scores in the final four GPs allowed Piquet to get back on terms, and when turbocharger failure brought Prost to a halt on lap 36 of the South African Grand Prix season closer, his quest for a first world title was over.

Cheever was third at Spa, a distant second in Canada and third again in Monza, but it was not the level of success the American was hoping for when he moved from Ligier. However, his start in the Dutch Grand Prix, where he vaulted from 11th on the grid to enter the first corner in second, is rightly remembered as one of the best ever seen in an era where getting the cars off the line was notoriously tricky!

Williams
FW08C & FW09

The headline-grabbing change to the regulations that the FISA Executive Committee announced on 14 October 1982 was the introduction of the full flat bottom, a move that effectively banned ground effect. But further down the 13-point list there was also another rule change that eliminated at least one of the cars planned for the 1983 season.

Point 12 banned the use of cars with more than four wheels. In the history of Formula 1, only the six-wheeled Tyrrell P34, which was campaigned in 1976 and 1977, had taken advantage of the previous loophole, but for 1983 that was going to change.

The P34 had two small front wheels on either side in a move that was designed to increase the amount of front-end grip while at the same time reducing the aerodynamic drag created by the front wheels. What Williams intended with the FW08B was very different. This car, which tested extensively during the 1982 season, had two regular-size front wheels – one on each side – but it had four full-size rear wheels.

All four rear wheels were driven in order to

LEFT Rosberg was in inspired form in the FW08C at Monaco, taking his only win of the season.
(John Townsend)

improve traction. The concept had first been trialled by the team on the FW07D of 1979. That car was considered too heavy, but when the concept was refined on the FW08 of 1982 the results were impressive, with Williams test driver Jonathan Palmer describing the traction out of slow corners as 'phenomenal'.

But with the 'B' banned, Williams elected to start the season with the conventional, four-wheel FW08C, which was a logical development of the car that took Keke Rosberg to the 1982 World Championship title. Other than Brabham, Williams was the only other team that arrived in Brazil for the opening race of the season with a car able to be refuelled mid-race, although, unlike the Brabham, it had a full-size tank so that the team had the option of not stopping.

Other than the new floor, the other main change was a shortening of the sidepods. Aside from that the car retained the aluminium honeycomb monocoque, the suspension was the same double-wishbone set-up at front and rear with coil springs over dampers and anti-roll bars at both ends.

The engine was an upgraded version of the venerable Cosworth DFV 3.5-litre V8, the DFY, prepared by engine specialist John Judd. The team ran a conventional Hewland five-speed FGA 400 gearbox and the engine ran on Mobil fuel. Goodyear supplied the tyres.

Alongside Rosberg, the team hired veteran Frenchman Jacques Laffite, who had previously driven for the team in 1974 and 1975. Rosberg started the season by setting

pole position for the Brazilian GP, and, light on fuel, he scorched away to lead the early laps. He was eventually caught and passed by Piquet, but was in a comfortable second place when he pitted to refuel.

As the hose was detached some fuel spilled onto the car and burst into flames. Rosberg instantly hopped from the car while the flames were extinguished. The car was undamaged and he jumped back in and raced his way back into second only to be disqualified for receiving a push start.

Laffite led briefly during a strong showing on his way to fourth place in round two at Long Beach but it was becoming clear that the normally aspirated cars were now no match for their turbocharged rivals. An inspired decision by Rosberg to start the Monaco Grand Prix on slick tyres despite the wet track was rewarded by a sensational win. He took advantage of the DFY's responsiveness at Detroit to take second place on the last day that the 'atmo' runners held sway over their blown rivals.

For the final race of the season Williams introduced the FW09. Designed by Patrick Head and Neil Oatley, with aerodynamics by Frank Dernie, the car was visually very different from the FW08C but it was what was under the bodywork that was the more significant alteration.

Ahead of the season Frank Williams had signed a deal with Honda for a supply of turbo engines, and the FW09 was the first Williams to carry the 1.5-litre 80-degree

RIGHT Laffite puts the Honda-powered FW09 through its paces at Kyalami.
(John Townsend)

V6. Based on Honda's successful Formula 2 powerplant, the RA163-E engine had twin KKK turbochargers and used Honda's in-house electronic fuel injection.

The car itself carried on with the use of aluminium honeycomb but the suspension was different from that of the FW08C, with a rocker-operated inboard damper used at the front and pullrod suspension at the rear. The transmission was a Williams six-speed design with Hewland internals.

Rosberg qualified sixth and Laffite tenth on the car's début. Laffite was forced off the track and into retirement on lap two by Eddie Cheever, but Rosberg finished fifth. It was a low-key start for a relationship that would go on to dominate Formula 1 in just a few seasons' time…

McLaren
MP4/1C & MP4/1E

Although it had never planned a six-wheeler, in many ways McLaren's 1983 season was similar to Williams' experience. It ran for most of the year using a Cosworth-powered car derived from the previous season's while its turbo-powered successor was waiting in the wings – with a big future ahead of it.

McLaren had introduced carbonfibre monocoques to Formula 1 in 1981 with the John Barnard-designed MP4. This concept had been refined and evolved to the MP4B for 1982, which in turn became the MP4/1C for 1983. Aside from the mandated floor changes and the shorter sidepods that followed in turn, the main difference was the adoption of pullrod suspension at the front.

The car retained the Hewland five-speed FGA 400 gearbox, Michelin tyres and Cosworth engine of its predecessors. The driver line-up of Niki Lauda and John Watson was carried over from 1982.

Watson and Lauda famously charged through the field from 22nd and 23rd on the grid to finish first and second respectively at Long Beach – still the lowest starting position from which a Formula 1 race has been won – for the team's high-point of the season.

Watson was third in Detroit as Cosworth-powered cars swept the podium on the stop/start street track and he claimed the 20th and final podium of his career with a solid drive to third place in the Dutch Grand Prix. That race in Zandvoort was where Lauda gave a début to the Porsche-engined turbo-powered MP4/1E.

But while the engine was designed and built by Porsche, it was badged as a TAG in deference to the team's sponsor, which funded the creation of the twin-turbo V6. In order to comply with Barnard's specifications, the TTE PO1 featured a 90-degree angle rather than the flat configuration that Porsche had used to great success in sports cars.

Other than the engine installation, the MP4/1E was effectively the same as the 1C. It was Lauda's perseverance that resulted in the car making its début mid-season, with Barnard allegedly reluctant to introduce the new engine until it had proved to be reliable. The British design legend may have had a point, but it was brake failure rather than an engine issue that brought the car's first appearance to an end.

A second turbo car was available for Watson at the next race at Monza, but this time it was two engine failures that ended the McLaren charge. Another engine failure accounted for

ABOVE The Porsche
turbo-powered
MP4/1E starred in
the season finale at
Kyalami.
(John Townsend)

Lauda at the European GP at Brands, while a
broken rear wing ensured that Watson ended
his 150th GP in the catch fencing.

Watson's bad run continued as he was
disqualified from the season-ending South African
GP after he was last away on the dummy grid yet
repassed the field to take up his original place on
the grid. Lauda was fastest in the warm-up, which
was a hint at what was to follow in the race.

The Austrian quickly worked his way from
12th on the grid into second place. Any hopes
of chasing down Piquet in the lead were hobbled
by a stuck wheel in the pit-stop, but he was back
into the top three when an electrical fault caused
him to stop with six laps remaining. But it had
been a small preview of how the McLaren-TAG
partnership would perform in 1984…

Alfa Romeo
183T

The main difference between Gérard
Ducarouge's Alfa Romeo 183T and the car that
preceded it – the 182 – was the engine. Gone
was the 3.5-litre V12 that Alfa had built for
Brabham to replace the previous flat-12 in order
to take full advantage of ground effect in 1979,
and in came a V8 twin-turbo the company had
been developing since 1980.

The engine had made a one-off appearance
at practice at the Italian GP in 1982. That
engine, the 890T, featured a 90-degree vee,
Sylo turbochargers, Marelli/Weber engine
management and ran on Agip fuel.

The chassis of the 183T was very similar
to the 1982 car, even down to the full-length

RIGHT De Cesaris
starred at Spa in the
Alfa Romeo 183T and
could have won the
race if the car hadn't
failed him.
(John Townsend)

sidepods, which were retained and housed the water and oil radiators. The suspension was a revised version of the set-up of lower wishbone/top rocker arms activating inboard spring/damper units front and rear.

The monocoque was carbonfibre and fabricated in the UK. The V8 turbo was a thirsty beast and the 183T started the season with a 250-litre fuel tank. After Alfa followed Brabham's lead and adopted mid-race refuelling, a revised car with a smaller tank was introduced for the British Grand Prix.

As was the case in 1982, Alfa ran on Michelin tyres, while Italian driver Andrea de Cesaris stayed with the team. He was joined by Mauro Baldi, who switched from Arrows. From his Formula 3 days Baldi was well known to the Euroracing team, which had taken over the running of the Alfa cars from the in-house Autodelta operation.

The drivers usually qualified on the fringes of the top ten, but it was not until Monaco that the team scored a point thanks to Baldi's sixth place. This made it all the more surprising when de Cesaris leaped off the line from third on the grid to lead at Spa.

He was more than seven seconds ahead when he pitted to refuel. A long stop dropped him to sixth, but any hope of a comeback was halted when his engine blew at the top of Eau Rouge a few laps later. Fastest lap was his sole consolation.

The power of the Alfa engine was demonstrated at Hockenheim, where de Cesaris again lined up third. His start was less stellar

this time, but in a race of attrition the Alfa held together and he took second place, a result he repeated in the season finale in South Africa.

Tyrrell
011 & 012

Ken Tyrrell's team started the season with a revised version of Maurice Philippe's 011 that had first raced in 1981. With an aluminium monocoque mated to double wishbones and the classic Cosworth DFY/Hewland gearbox combination, the Goodyear-shod car was driven by Michele Alboreto and American Danny Sullivan.

The all-green Benetton-liveried car scored two points finishes, the first a fifth place at Spa thanks to Sullivan, the second a brilliant, if unlikely, win at Detroit in the hands of Alboreto.

Not only would this turn out to be the 33rd and final Tyrrell win, it would also be the 155th and last for the DFV (albeit it in DFY configuration) after a remarkable service that began in 1967.

At the Austrian Grand Prix, Alboreto gave Philippe's 012 its début. This car was the first Tyrrell to feature carbonfibre in the monocoque, although, like the Brabham, aluminium honeycomb was still a significant part of its construction. Pullrod suspension was introduced all round and Tyrrell brought in its own gearbox design, which incorporated the oil tank.

The 012 had very short, BT52-esque sidepods, while the shape of the rear wing was a most unusual inverted V. Alboreto qualified 0.7s quicker than Sullivan in the 011 on the car's début, but crashed out of the race. He scored a point next time out in Holland with sixth place. Sullivan had the 012 for the final two races, but there were no more top-six finishes.

Lotus
92, 93T & 94T
The death of the inspirational Lotus founder Colin Chapman during the winter of 1982 had an understandably seismic effect on the team. Chapman had secured a supply of Renault turbo engines before his death and together with Martin Ogilvie he designed the 93T – the first turbo-powered Lotus Formula 1 car.

But initially Renault had only agreed to supply one car, so while Elio de Angelis was getting used to turbo power, Nigel Mansell was entrusted with the 92. This was the last Lotus designed for the Cosworth DFV and it was an evolution of the previous year's 91, which meant a carbonfibre and Kevlar monocoque and Hewland five-speed gearbox.

There was one area where the car was very different – the 92 had computer-controlled 'active' suspension. This employed hydraulic jacks rather than conventional suspension components, and was designed to give the car a self-levelling ride and maximise cornering ability. The other big change was the switch from Goodyear to Pirelli radial tyres.

Mansell managed just a single top-six finish in the 92, taking a point at Detroit. From the British Grand Prix onwards he drove the turbo car and the active-suspension programme was put on the back burner. It made a race-winning return in 1987 on the bright yellow 99T.

BELOW Mansell started the season with the Cosworth-powered 92 and its 'active' suspension. It was not a success.
(John Townsend)

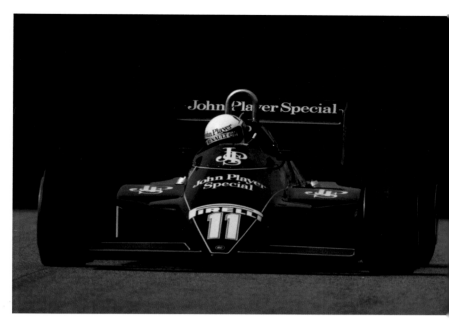

The 93T had the same monocoque, used double wishbones and pullrod suspension, and was powered, of course, by Renault's Formula 1 V6 turbo. It was not a success, however. Although de Angelis was occasionally able to qualify the car in the top ten (he started fourth in Detroit), he managed just a single finish, a lapped ninth at Spa.

Gérard Ducarouge had been fired by Alfa Romeo only a month into the season and was snapped up by Team Lotus principal Peter Warr to turn around the team's fortunes. The Frenchman was given just six weeks to come up with the 94T, which made its début at the British Grand Prix.

The monocoque was slimmer and lighter, but in order to house the radiators and intercoolers the car still retained full-length sidepods. The suspension was a wholesale change, with rocker arms employed at the front and pullrods at the rear.

The 94T was instantly more competitive than its predecessor, with Mansell finishing fourth on its début. He was fifth in Austria, as was de Angelis in Italy, while at the European GP at Brands de Angelis put the Lotus on pole and Mansell delighted the crowd in the race, setting the fastest lap and producing a charging drive to third place.

BELOW **Gérard Ducarouge's 94T returned Lotus to pole position for the first time since 1978.** (*John Townsend*)

Toleman
TG183B

Toleman produced one of the most striking-looking cars of the 1983 season with the Rory Byrne-designed TG183B. Retaining only the double wishbone and pullrod front suspension and carbonfibre/Kevlar monocoque from the TG183 of 1982, its new car was the philosophical opposite of the BT52. The contrast stemmed from the front end. Murray had worked hard to move as much weight to the rear as possible in the Brabham. Byrne on the other hand created a bulky, full-width nose section that housed oil and water radiators.

Further back, he also took the rules to the limit by introducing a twin rear wing. This incorporated massive endplates that linked the two wings, one that ran ahead of the rear axle, and one aft of it at the very maximum permitted by the rules.

At the rear end double wishbones were connected to pushrods and spring/damper units. As had been the case since Toleman entered Formula 1 in 1981, the engine was Brian Hart's Hart 415T, straight-four, 1.5-litre turbocharged unit. This was mated to a standard Hewland five-speed gearbox, Garrett AiResearch turbo and ran on Agip fuel.

Pirelli tyres were carried over from 1982 and so was lead driver Derek Warwick. The team had initially planned to enter just a single car, but when Bruno Giacomelli was released by Alfa, he was drafted in to create a two-car line-up.

Toleman was the surprise of pre-season testing when Warwick was fastest as all the teams gathered in Rio ahead of the first race. This promise was converted into fifth on the grid for the season opener, but he ended the race a lap down in eighth place after a brief grassy excursion following a tangle with Alfa's Mauro Baldi.

That set the tone for the opening half of the season, but at the Dutch Grand Prix Warwick finished fourth, which started a run of four consecutive points finishes, and included a double score in the European GP, where Warwick was fifth and Giacomelli took his only point of the year in sixth.

Arrows
A6

The biggest news at Arrows was that it had signed 1980 World Champion Alan Jones to drive in 1983, although the Australian would have to miss the start of the season as he was recovering from a broken leg after being thrown from a horse.

The A6 was a logical development of the A5 the team introduced for the final three races of 1982. The Dave Wass-designed car had an aluminium monocoque as the unsponsored team could not afford a carbonfibre version.

As was the case with every Arrows to date, the car was fitted with the Cosworth V8 – in this instance the DFY, a revised version of the DFV

that revved higher – and Hewland gearbox. It ran on Valvoline fuel and Goodyear tyres.

With Jones injured, Marc Surer was partnered by Chico Serra for the Brazilian GP. Jones returned for the Race of Champions at Brands Hatch and finished third. He made his GP début for Arrows at Long Beach, where he qualified 12th (four spots ahead of Surer) but his time away from the cockpit since his retirement at the end of 1981 meant he was not race-fit and he had to withdraw after 59 laps.

Jones would never be seen in an Arrows again. Serra initially returned to the team, but for the Belgian GP Thierry Boutsen raised

sufficient sponsorship ($50,000) to secure the ride and remained with the team for the rest of the season.

Surer started the season with three top-six finishes in the opening four races, but neither he nor any of his team-mates troubled the scorers again as the turbo cars came into their own.

Theodore
N183
Over the closed season Theodore merged with Mo Nunn's Ensign team and for 1983 the team campaigned the N183 that Nigel Bennett had designed for Ensign.

ABOVE Thierry Boutsen brought much-needed sponsorship to Arrows when he arrived mid-season.
(John Townsend)

LEFT Theodore campaigned the N183 that was initially designed for Ensign.
(John Townsend)

RIGHT The Ligier
JS21 featured Citroën-
based hydraulic
suspension, but was
an uncompetitive car.
(John Townsend)

Despite money being exceptionally tight, the monocoque did feature some carbonfibre alongside aluminium honeycomb. The biggest change was the switch from Avon tyres to Michelin.

South American drivers Johnny Cecotto and Roberto Guerrero were hired to race and the former drove brilliantly to take sixth place and a point at Long Beach. But that was the only time the team made it into the points all season. Cecotto left after the Italian GP and the team folded one race later.

Ligier
JS21

With Matra abandoning its plans to build a V6 turbo and team boss Guy Ligier deciding a supply of Renault turbo units was too expensive, Ligier reverted to Cosworth and its revised normally aspirated DFY for 1983.

Michel Beaujon and Claude Galopin designed the JS21, the car on the grid that most closely aped the concept of the BT52, with a heavily rear-biased weight distribution and no sidepods. The team retained the aluminium honeycomb monocoque from the JS19 of 1982 and the *de rigueur* Hewland FGB five-speed gearbox.

The JS21 did have one very novel feature – Citroën-based hydraulic suspension. This used a belt-driven pump to maintain the car's ride height. The car ran on Elf fuel and Michelin tyres.

Experienced French driver Jean-Pierre Jarier was recruited to partner young Brazilian Raul Boesel. Jarier was in inspired form at Long Beach, qualifying tenth and racing into the battle for the lead until a collision with Rosberg took both out.

After that neither he nor Boesel ever troubled the scorers and for the first time in its history Ligier failed to score a point during an entire season.

Spirit
201 & 201C

Spirit was the only new team to enter Formula 1 in 1983. Founded by Gordon Coppuck and John Wickham in 1981, Spirit enjoyed a strong first season in Formula 2, winning three races and taking third in the standings with Thierry Boutsen driving its Honda-powered 201 chassis.

Honda was keen to return to Formula 1 for the first time since 1968, but wanted to keep a low profile as it developed its RA163E V6 turbo engine, which was based on the race-winning Formula 2 powerplant. Thus Spirit was entrusted with the project and developed a version of its 201 Formula 2 car as a test mule.

The 201 was a conventional car with an aluminium monocoque and double-wishbone suspension. Using Goodyear tyres and Shell fuel, the Spirit-Honda made its race début at the Race of Champions. After qualifying on the

last row, Stefan Johansson retired with a blown engine after just four laps.

Designed by Coppuck and John Baldwin, the 201C featured a longer wheelbase, revised bodywork and suspension, and the team's in-house cast-magnesium oil tank/bellhousing. The new car was supposed to give the team its full Formula 1 début at the British GP, but it developed an engine problem that meant Johansson had to take to the test-hack 201. Nevertheless he qualified an encouraging 14th but retired when the fuel pump failed.

The 201C finally made its début in Germany and Johansson again qualified encouragingly in 13th place. This time it was engine failure that ended his race. A misfire in the warm-up meant Johansson had to revert to the 201 for the Austrian GP, but he did at least manage to get to the finish, taking the flag five laps down in 12th place. He was back in the 201C for the Dutch GP and just missed out on a point in seventh.

The team had been working on a bespoke Formula 1 chassis, the 101, and took it to the Italian GP at Monza despite it not being finished. This car featured an all-new monocoque, revised engine installation and better aerodynamics. The aim was to complete the car at the race, but when engine problems struck the older car, this work never took place and the newcomer did not run. The 101 then appeared at the European GP at Brands but overheating problems meant that it ran only briefly in practice.

ABOVE The Spirit 201 was effectively an F2 car, but it brought Honda's V6 turbo into F1. *(John Townsend)*

The Monza debacle is often credited with convincing Honda to pull the plug on the Spirit partnership and concentrate solely on supporting Williams for the 1984 season.

BELOW The 201C was a refinement of Spirit's F2 chassis, but didn't score a point. *(John Townsend)*

RIGHT The ATS D5 was the first all-carbon F1 car, but poor reliability meant it wasn't a success. *(John Townsend)*

ATS

D6

While John Barnard is rightly credited with introducing carbonfibre into Formula 1 chassis design with the MP4 of 1981, that car's monocoque and that of the many imitations it spawned still featured some element of aluminium honeycomb in the construction.

The first Formula 1 car to have a chassis made completely of carbonfibre was produced by Günter Schmid's ATS team in the shape of the D6 created by Gustav Brunner for the 1983 season. Team ATS entered Formula 1 in 1977 and through to 1982 it had always run the Cosworth DFV engine. But for the 1983 season Schmid used his connections in Germany to secure a supply of BMW M12/13 turbo engines.

Manfred Winkelhock was the sole driver of the single-car entry, which ran on Goodyear tyres and used Shell fuel. ATS developed its own gearbox, which employed Hewland five-speed internals.

BELOW Tony Southgate's Osella FA1E (seen here with Piercarlo Ghinzani at the wheel) drew on the lessons learned from the BT52, with short sidepods and a rearward weight bias. *(LAT)*

Although the car often ran well in qualifying, with Winkelhock regularly starting inside the top ten, reliability was poor. In fact the German only made it to the chequered flag on four occasions and failed to score any points. The nadir came at the German GP at Hockenheim when a broken turbo pipe ruled Winkelhock out of Friday qualifying, which meant that when it rained during Saturday's session he failed to qualify for his and the team's home race.

Osella
FA1D, FA1E
This tiny Italian team started the season with a revised version of Giorgio Valentini's Cosworth-powered FA1D that it had campaigned in 1982. The team switched from Pirelli to Michelin tyres, but this did not help Piercarlo Ghinzani, who failed to qualify for all three races in which he used the car.

For the Detroit round, the Italian driver had the Tony Southgate-designed FA1E at his disposal. This had the Alfa Romeo V12 1260 engine that the factory team had abandoned in favour of its turbo unit. The car featured the aluminium honeycomb monocoque from the FA1D, but had shorter sidepods and looked altogether a much more modern racer.

Corrado Fabi, the team's other driver, had to wait until the British GP before he had the FA1E and secured the team's best result of the season when he took tenth place in Austria. Ghinzani managed to qualify the new car seven times, but only made the finish once, which was also in Austria, where he was 11th.

March-RAM
01
John MacDonald's RAM team ran Dave Kelly's RAM 01 chassis for a number of drivers during the 1983 season but qualified for just three races.

Using the updated version of the Cosworth DFV engine, the DFY, and the Hewland FG400 gearbox, the car featured an aluminium monocoque with glassfibre bodywork. It had double wishbones with coil springs over dampers at both ends. It ran on Pirelli tyres.

Eliseo Salazar managed to get it on the grid for the first two races but quit the team after the Belgian GP. Jean-Louis Schlesser failed to qualify in a one-off appearance in a second car at the French GP. After the team skipped Detroit, Jacques Villeneuve attempted to qualify for his home race in Canada but failed.

Irishman Kenny Acheson saw out the second half of the season at RAM, finally making it onto the grid in South Africa and getting to the flag in 12th place, six laps down.

BELOW RAM's 01 was a rare sight in grands prix, as a series of drivers struggled to get it through qualifying.
(John Townsend)

Index